Presbyterian Creeds

Books by Jack Rogers
Published by The Westminster Press

Presbyterian Creeds:
A Guide to The Book of Confessions

Confessions of a Conservative Evangelical

In collaboration with Ross Mackenzie and Louis Weeks

Case Studies in Christ and Salvation

Presbyterian Creeds

A Guide to The Book of Confessions

Jack Rogers

With a foreword by Charles A. Hammond

The Westminster Press
Philadelphia

Book design by Gene Harris

First edition

Published by The Westminster Press®
Philadelphia, Pennsylvania

PRINTED IN THE UNITED STATES OF AMERICA

9 8 7 6 5 4 3 2 1

Dedicated to the memory of
Addison H. Leitch
President
and the faculty of
Pittsburgh-Xenia Seminary
1955–1959
who taught and modeled
a unity of faith and practice

Library of Congress Cataloging in Publication Data
Rogers, Jack Bartlett.
Presbyterian creeds.
1. Presbyterian Church—Creeds—History. 2. Creeds—History. I. Title.
BX9183.R59 1985 238'.5137 84-22001
ISBN 0-664-24627-3 (pbk.)

Contents

Foreword
by Charles A. Hammond

Do you have to believe anything to be a Presbyterian?

What a strange question. Of course you do. All religious communities are formed essentially of those who have similar beliefs about reality. By definition, to be a worshipping, praying, serving community is to hold in common certain beliefs about who it is we worship, to whom we pray, and why and how we serve. Of course being a Presbyterian means to believe something.

In strictly constitutional terms (and we Presbyterians like constitutions), "One becomes an active member of the church through faith in Jesus Christ as Savior and acceptance of his Lordship in all of life" (G-5.0101). To be an officer of the Presbyterian Church is to believe more specifically. It is to express that belief within certain historic formulations and to be guided and instructed by a particular collection of belief statements called *The Book of Confessions.*

Do you have to believe anything to be a Presbyterian? Of course.

But how could you know this, considering the lack of discussion, lack of material, and lack of familiarity with and regular use of this repository of beliefs? In 1967, the former United Presbyterian Church in the United States of America adopted a collection of nine confessions as its central theological resource. Since that time, little has been done to educate the people in the church as to the contents of that book or its implications. A few useful tools have been developed here and there by concerned individuals, some work has been done on particular confessions, but there has been no churchwide educational program.

In the mid-seventies the former Presbyterian Church in the United States held a lengthy conversation throughout the whole church as it debated a possible new statement of faith. But in the time since the Plan for Reunion was first proposed, with a book of confessions included as part of the plan (nearly four years now), nothing has been done to help Presbyterians, north, east, south, or west, come to know and understand the convictions we claim ought to direct our worship and our service.

"Our service": There is the key to the matter. The entire life of our church's witness in the world—in justice ministries, in peacemaking, in seeking inclusiveness and working for equality of persons—depends on what we believe. In a historic judicial case that dealt with the matter of the ordination of women elders, it was clearly shown upon what our ministry is based. The Permanent Judicial Commission said, in the case of *Maxwell et al. v. the Presbytery of Pittsburgh*, "Our form of government must be inseparably connected to the faith we profess. The question of the importance of our belief in the equality of people before God is thus essential" (*Minutes of the General Assembly*, UPCUSA, 1975, p. 257).

All our attempts to witness to the liberating power of the gospel mean nothing if we believe nothing about the gospel, the love of God, and the presence of the Spirit in the church and the world. The rush of the younger members of our culture after neo-fundamentalist movements, pseudo-eastern religions, and personality-based cults is a sign that we have not articulated to our own children the beliefs we claim to share and that motivate our witness and service in the world.

After a decade of faithful service to the Presbyterian Church at the national level, trying to help us apply our beliefs to the issue of inclusive language and to the question of biblical authority, Professor Jack Rogers, who has written major works on the Westminster Confession and the history of biblical authority in our tradition, now offers us help in remedying what Dr. James I. McCord, Chancellor of the Center of Theological Inquiry at Princeton Theological Seminary, called the church's "theological amnesia."

Here, using the case-study method so admirably developed for theological study during the last fifteen years, Dr. Rogers gives us a useful and thorough introduction to *The Book of Confessions.* Putting theological discussion in concrete situations, with some literary license to help get us involved, he gives us a historical approach to each confession, as well as its important focus and its relevance to the contemporary scene.

The relationship Dr. Rogers highlights between *The Book of Confessions,* the new wording of the questions asked at ordination and installation, and Chapter II of *The Book of Order,* "The Church and Its Confessions," is most useful. The entire concept in the new questions of "essential tenets," while used first in slightly different form in the compromise phrased for the Adopting Act of 1729, has a most checkered history in our tradition and is alarming to some. The definition of basic themes, in light of *The Book of Order* and of highlights of Catholic, Reformation, and, particularly, Reformed doctrines, will help us to keep this phrase from becoming schismatic and lead us to a more holistic use of the unity between confession and polity.

Dr. Rogers also serves on the committee recently formed to prepare a new statement of the Reformed faith for the reunited church. Do you have to believe anything to be a Presbyterian? Of course, for if we are not willing to spend time struggling with our own confessional tradition, then the labors of that committee will be useless. We can remember that one of the oldest phrases in our Constitution reads, "Truth is in order to goodness . . . and no opinion can be either more pernicious or more absurd than that which brings truth and falsehood upon a level, and represents it as of no consequence what a [person's] opinions are" (G-1.0304).

It is my earnest hope that the whole church, during the years it will take that worthy group of elders, pastors, scholars, authors, and theologians to draft a contemporary statement of the Reformed faith, will be prepared for a productive debate on its contents by learning the history of our Reformed tradition represented in the confessions. Professor Rogers's study will help us in that task. I would welcome any additions to the library of resources this book begins. The thematic approach of Dr. William Keesecker's study for laypersons is useful to many, and one could hope that Dr. Harry Eberts's essays on the confessions might be collected and distributed in one book. But for now I encourage you to be open to the introduction given by Jack Rogers. May it lead to increased study of the confessions and to increased faithfulness in service inspired by commitment to the "essential tenets of the Reformed faith."

Preface

For the past five years I have used John Leith's *Introduction to the Reformed Tradition,* along with Edward A. Dowey, Jr.'s, *A Commentary on the Confession of 1967 and an Introduction to "The Book of Confessions,"* as texts for my course in Presbyterian Ethos. Both books have been of great benefit to me and to my students.

What neither of these books did was to detail the historical background in which the confessions in our *Book of Confessions* developed. For that I developed my own syllabus of case studies, or historical narratives, of the context of the confessions, using the technique of "case writing" developed and taught at the Harvard Business School.

Part of my joy and responsibility over the years has been involving students and others in researching and writing about the confessions using the case-study method. I have encouraged students to believe that their work could contribute to the learning of others and might eventually appear in published form. This is the fulfillment of that promise for many students. For this book I have added to, redesigned, and rewritten the cases that grew from our group effort. I take responsibility for remaining inadequacies in both style and content, but I remain pleased with this fruit of cooperative academic endeavor.

Special thanks are due to several persons. The first "case" I ever wrote was one on the Council of Nicaea in collaboration with Ross Mackenzie. Some of that material in revised form appears in the chapter on the Nicene Creed. Professor Henry Ferry of Howard University in Washington, D.C., provided a perspective from the nation's capital on the case of the Confession of 1967. For part of one academic year, Julia Hastings was employed by Fuller Theological Seminary as a program assistant in the Office of Field Education and was seconded to assist me part-time in the Office of Presbyterian Ministries. A major part of her assignment was to assist in pulling together material from cases written by students and incorporating them into my syllabus, "Case Studies in the Reformed Confessions." During the academic years 1983–84 and 1984–85, Carol Howard assisted me in the Office of Presbyterian Ministries. Her considerable skills and her willingness to assume extra responsibility and protect me from interruption were major factors in enabling me to finish this book.

My wife, Sharee, and my three sons, Matthew, John, and Toby, shared significantly in this venture. Sharee and Matthew read the entire manuscript and made helpful criticisms of both style and substance. As always I remain thankful to my family as my primary community of support and encouragement.

I have the privilege of being one of the twenty-one members appointed by Moderator J. Randolph Taylor to the Special Committee on a Brief Statement of the Reformed Faith for possible inclusion in *The Book of Confessions.* My commitment to and conception of this book long predates the creation of that committee, and the manuscript was finished well before the Special Committee began its substantial work. The Committee met on May 24 and 25, 1984, in Chicago, to be constituted and charged by Moderator Taylor, to begin to become acquainted, and to clear some common dates for future meetings. I make reference to that meeting, and Dr. Taylor's charge, in chapter 1. Nothing else in the book is in response to the Committee's work. I look forward to growth in my own understanding of the creeds, confessions, catechisms, and theological declarations of the Reformed tradition through my work on the Committee. This book is one small contribution to what I hope will be a comprehensive process involving the whole of the Presbyterian Church (U.S.A.) in thinking about our theological heritage as we move toward confessing our faith anew in the 1980s.

Rosh Hashana, 1984

JACK ROGERS
Director, Office of Presbyterian Ministries
and
Professor of Philosophical Theology
Fuller Theological Seminary
Pasadena, California

Tenets of the Reformed Faith

Confession	*Date/Country*	*Historical Context*	*Contrasting View*
Nicene Creed	4th C. Middle East	Unifying Constantine's empire	Arians
Apostles' Creed	2nd to 9th C. France	Baptism of new Christians	Greek gods and Roman emperor worship
Scots Confession	1560 Scotland	Scottish civil war	Medieval Catholicism
Heidelberg Catechism	1563 Germany	Breaking the Peace of Augsburg	Lutherans
Second Helvetic Confession	1566 Switzerland	Black plague and help for Heidelberg	Anabaptists
Westminster Confession and Catechisms	1647 England	English civil war	High Church Anglicans
Barmen Declaration	1934 Germany	Nazism	Nationalism
Confession of 1967	1967 United States	Civil rights movement	Civil religion

Compiled by Jack Rogers, 1984

Expressed in the Confessions of Our Church

Central Doctrine	*Theologian*	*Symbol*
The Person of Jesus Christ The reality of the Holy Spirit	Athanasius	
One God in three persons Creator of heaven and earth	Unknown	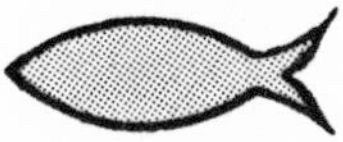
Election The church	Knox	
Stewardship The Lord's Supper	Ursinus and Olevianus	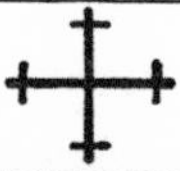
Covenant Baptism	Bullinger	
The sovereignty of God The authority and interpretation of Scripture	Reynolds	
The sin of idolatry The Lordship of Christ	Barth	
Reconciliation The equality of all persons	Dowey	

BO G-14.0405c; G-2.000–2.0500

1

A Church That Defines and Affirms Its Faith

Our church has a "Book of Confessions": historic statements, or creeds, that proclaim what we believe. Why do we have them? Do we still need them? What does it mean when we "confess," or profess, our faith publicly? These are questions Presbyterians are discussing today.

At the reuniting General Assembly of the Presbyterian Church (U.S.A.) in 1983, a Task Force on the Confessional Nature of the Church held open hearings on these questions. A former Moderator of the General Assembly asked, "How can candidates for ordination receive the essential tenets [beliefs] of the Reformed faith before they know what those tenets are?" A denominational executive lamented, "We need to point to the distressing reality that there is biblical amnesia." A seminary professor observed, "We have a great illiteracy regarding our confessional tradition." A pastor pleaded, "We have all but lost our confessional identity. What does it mean to be a Reformed Christian?" And a layperson declared, "The average church member wants to know the difference between Christian and non-Christian, and what the distinctives of the Presbyterian denomination are."

The Challenge of a New Confession

The reuniting General Assembly in 1983 directed its newly elected Moderator, Dr. J. Randolph Taylor, to "appoint a committee representing diversities of points of view and groups within the reunited church to prepare a Brief Statement of the Reformed Faith for possible inclusion in *The Book of Confessions.*" This was in accordance with the Articles of Agreement that led to the reunion. Two reasons were given for this action. The first was the need of the reunited church to give to the world a clear testimony of its faith as a confessing Reformed church. The second was the concern that the church's beliefs be declared while the direction of the church's mission was being set. Apparently the commissioners to that historic General Assembly believed that articulating the church's faith in a confessional statement was integral both to the identity and to the mission of the church.

In 1984, Moderator Taylor appointed a twenty-one-person committee. In May of that year, he met with them and clarified their mandate. He spoke of a moment in which the future of the church could be shaped. The clay, which would soon harden, was yet wet. "Only once in a century," he said, "do we get to raise such fundamental questions as Who are we? What do we value? What are we going to do about it?" For Taylor, there were five goals for the committee to pursue:

1. Help the church recapture and reassert its identity as the people of God. This identity, for him, was more than just a common form of church government.

2. Introduce and reintroduce our own particular tradition in the theological family. Church members, he knew, were very likely to come from a non-Reformed background. There was a need to identify the particular contribution made by the Reformed tradition.

3. Challenge the church to theological discussion. There must be theological fellowship with a diversity which has creativity.

4. Help the church focus on essentials. What do we believe? And where should we focus attention in the 1980s?

5. Call the church to the meaning of affirmations. "Who

are we as a community created by the grace of God?" Taylor asked. "Discover what it is to be a confessing church," he exhorted.

Are We Reformed?

In 1984 and 1985 every governing body of the Presbyterian Church (U.S.A.), from session through presbytery and synod to General Assembly, was invited to contribute to the Design for Mission of the new denomination. The data from this extensive survey are the material from which decisions about the mission and structure of the new denomination are drawn. It is equally important that every member, and especially every church officer, contribute to the rethinking of the theological identity of the church. According to *The Book of Order* (*BO* G-2.0100), it is in our confessional statements that the church declares to its members and to the world who and what it is, what it believes, and what it resolves to do. Confessional issues are issues of the identity of a community. If we are to be one church we must learn to discuss theology, to say clearly what we believe. To do that we must know where we have come from, who we are today, and where we mean to go in the future. We can no longer assume that the phrase "the Reformed tradition" carries a common meaning for Presbyterian church members.

The Task Force on Biblical Authority and Interpretation of the former United Presbyterian Church in the U.S.A. discovered this through a survey conducted by the Presbyterian Panel in 1980. Scientifically selected panelists represented a cross-section of persons in the denomination. They were asked which of several views regarding Scripture they thought most nearly represented that of the Reformed tradition. About one third of those surveyed asked, in effect, "What is the Reformed tradition?" Another third said that they thought they knew and that they disagreed with it. A majority of the final third said that the Reformed tradition was what they had previously identified as their own position. It is disturbing that perhaps two thirds of Presbyterians, as indicated by this survey, either do not know or feel alienated from what they believe to be the confessional heritage of their church. There would appear to be a critical need to clarify the content of our confessional tradition.

A Swiss Reformation

The Task Force on Biblical Authority and Interpretation in its report to the 1982 General Assembly found it necessary to define the term "Reformed." They did so first by noting the time and place where this particular movement began.

The Reformed Protestant tradition began in Switzerland with Ulrich Zwingli at about the same time that Martin Luther was posting his ninety-five theses in Germany. This Swiss reformation spread to Eastern Europe and also up the Rhine, to the low countries, and across the channel to England and Scotland. It was perhaps Queen Elizabeth who dubbed this branch of the Protestant movement "Reformed." Because of their emphasis on simplicity of worship and discipline in public and private life, the Queen announced her judgment that the Swiss were "more Reformed" than the Lutherans. Luther was content simply to reject those matters of medieval doctrine, worship, or life which seemed to him marked clearly as wrong by the Word of God. Zwingli, Calvin, and the other Swiss Reformers took the opposite approach. They desired to reform all of life, in the church and in the world, and were willing to retain only those elements of doctrine, worship, and lifestyle for which they believed there was a positive basis in the Scriptures.

Thus the word "Reformed" refers to one branch of the Protestant reformation movement, which had a particular locale and history and, as we will see, developed some distinctive theological emphases.

How Do We Receive and Adopt?

It is time we put an end to the pious hypocrisy into which we force many, if not most, of the office-bearers in our church. All elders and deacons are required to take the same vow that ministers of the Word take with regard to the confessions of the church. At the time of their ordination, our lay officers are asked, "Do you sincerely receive and adopt the essential tenets of the Reformed faith as expressed in the confessions of our church as authentic and reliable expositions of what Scripture leads us to believe and do, and will you be instructed and led by those confessions as you lead the people of God?"

It is surely difficult to receive and adopt essential tenets if no one has told you what they are. It is even more difficult to be instructed and led by the confessions if you have never studied them. It would probably be chilling to discover how few office-bearers of the church have ever been asked to take that vow seriously. This is not to criticize the lay leaders. Quite the opposite; they can hardly be held accountable for something their pastors have not taught them. And the pastors are hard-pressed to teach if there are no materials available to make these confessions from past times accessible to contemporary people. We are simply reaping the fruit of the "theological amnesia" of the past several decades.

Can We Be Reformed and Always Reforming?

Presbyterians hold two values in tension. One is the freedom of individual conscience, the other is the integrity of the community's standards. This tension is as old as American Presbyterianism. It represents our desire to be always reforming, granting freedom to those who seek to reform us. It equally represents our desire to be Reformed, maintaining a continuity with the past which has shaped our identity. We have been healthiest as a church when we have maintained a balance between these two values. In earlier centuries we have split along New Side/Old Side and New School/Old School lines when we have not been able to maintain the tension.

The balance between these two values has always been maintained in terms of a delicate compromise embodied in the Adopting Act of 1729. When the Westminster Confession of Faith and the Catechisms were adopted as the confessional standards of American Presbyterianism, office-bearers were asked to agree to the standards "as being, in all the essential and necessary articles, good forms of sound words and systems of Christian doctrine." The link between freedom of conscience and the integrity of the communty's standards was the notion of "essential and necessary articles." Freedom was allowed in nonessentials, and the standards were upheld in essentials.

The concept of "essential and necessary articles" fell on bad times during the Fundamentalist/Modernist controversy in the late nineteenth and early twentieth centuries. The dominant conservative party in 1910 enforced a selection of five articles from the Confession which were considered essential and necessary. These articles symbolized for many in the denomination an attempted imposition of a system of theology and biblical interpretation against which they protested. Severe polarization in the church led in 1927 to the report of a special theological commission and the General Assembly's ruling that no one, not even the General Assembly, should designate essential and necessary articles that definitively interpreted the Confession, except in application to specific judicial cases. This decision opened the present era of theological pluralism. It reflected a revulsion against theological conflict and heresy trials. Freedom of conscience had triumphed.

In the 1970s we discovered that we could not function without the concept of "essential and necessary articles." A young applicant for ordination argued that he could be a loyal Presbyterian without participating in the ordination of women because that was a "nonessential point in Presbyterianism." The Permanent Judicial Commission of the General Assembly declared, to the contrary, that "it is evident from our Church's confessional standards that the Church believes the Spirit of God has led us into new understandings of this equality before God." Now the integrity of standards was invoked and the concept of essential articles reintroduced.

The tension between freedom of conscience and the integrity of the community's standards is often difficult to sustain. But we are most whole when we do. The key is knowing what is essential.

Essential Tenets, or Beliefs

Our present *Book of Order* gives significant guidance on what it is essential to believe. In its Chapter II, "The Church and Its Confessions," the governmental handbook of our denomination is keyed to the theological heritage of the church. *The Book of Order* declares that the creeds and confessions of the church identify us as a community, guide us in studying Scripture, and summarize the essence of the Christian tradition. Thus, the confessions equip us for the task of proclaiming the good news. The chapter cautions us as to the serious nature of these subordinate standards, saying, "The church is prepared to counsel with or even to discipline one ordained who seriously rejects the faith expressed in the confessions." And it reminds us that a more exacting process is required to change the confessions than is needed to alter matters of government, discipline, or service.

The Book of Order then proceeds to list ten doctrines which we can take to be essential and necessary. Two are noted as shared with the church catholic, or universal: the mystery of the Trinity, and the incarnation of the eternal Word of God in Jesus Christ. Two are identified with our affirmation of the Protestant Reformation: justification by grace through faith, and Scripture as the final authority for salvation and the life of faith. Six are declared to express the faith of the Reformed tradition. (These are not exclusively the product or property of that branch of the Protestant tradition named Reformed. The desire of these Reformers was simply to recover the simplicity of Christianity as professed and practiced by the early church. But as they developed their understanding of the Christian faith in their own particular time, place, and context, they necessarily and understandably emphasized certain motifs more than others.) The six themes stated in *The Book of Order* as characteristic of the Reformed tradition are God's sovereignty; God's choosing (election) of people for salvation and service; the covenant life of the church, ordering itself according to the Word of God; a faithful stewardship of God's creation; the sin of idolatry, which makes anything created ultimate, rather than worshipping only the Creator; and the necessity of obedience to the Word of God, which directs us to work for justice in the transformation of society.

These ten doctrines are the result of prayer, thought, and experience within a living tradition reflecting on the Word of God. It is essential and necessary that Presbyterians understand, reflect on, and act out their convictions regarding Trinity, Incarnation, Justification, Scripture, Sovereignty, Election, Covenant, Stewardship, Sin, and Obedience.

Latitude Within Limits

The listing in *The Book of Order,* while not exhaustive, is helpful. It indicates that not everything in the confessions is of equal weight. Some things are more important, more characteristic, more useful for today than others. Since the confessions are outline guides to the main teachings of Scripture, it is important for us to develop an understanding of their essential tenets. A sound rule of biblical interpretation is that obscure and secondary elements are to be interpreted in light of the clear and central teachings. So with the confessions; it is necessary that we discern the central motifs and differentiate them from details which are related only to the cultural setting and theological situation of that particular time and place.

There is some latitude regarding what it is essential to believe and act upon. The confessions do not speak with one voice in the fashion of a seminary textbook in theology. Neither do they speak so diversely that nothing coherent and constructive emerges. There is a general harmony, a broad consensus, a functional unity to which we can appeal. The confessions pose helpful limits. They are useful in defining our roots in the Reformed community and the resources which that community uniquely has to offer in the ecumenical mix. The confessions also provide a latitude, even a demand, for us to confess our faith anew in every generation. There is yet more light to break forth, not just from our individual minds or our group experience but from the Word of God. It is to the seeking of that biblical light that the confessions continually direct us. It is by new insights gleaned from the Word of God that the Reformed community is to be continually reforming itself. Knowing the outline of what our forerunners in the faith felt to be central will free us to seek further depths, both of clarity and commitment.

Setting the Margins

A word processor or personal computer has preprogrammed margins, on the left and on the right. Within these margins, we have complete freedom to write what we want, changing and experimenting at will. We can also alter these margins, making them wider or narrower. But we cannot function without some kind of margin on either side. Neither can we in our denomination live peaceably together and move forward in mission unless we know what is essential and necessary for us and what is the area in which we have freedom of individual conscience. We need to be confessional—positively appropriating our Reformed heritage. Then we are free to be confessing—declaring our contemporary convictions, informed by Scripture, and reforming of the church and the world. That means that church members, and especially office-bearers, will function better as they become conscious of and comfortable with the "essential tenets of the Reformed faith as expressed in the confessions of our church." The purpose of this book is to provide a resource to help Presbyterians reach that goal.

2

From Scripture to Confessions of Faith

How do we get from the Bible to a written, formal statement of faith? Let us examine the normal, human, and necessary process that takes place. Choose a simple biblical statement such as "Our Father who art in heaven" (Matt. 6:9). That isn't even a complete sentence; it is just a phrase. And it is not meant as a creedal statement in the first instance. Jesus is teaching his disciples to pray. We, as Jesus' contemporary disciples, also pray that prayer. But we do more than pray. On occasion, when we are at our best, we also think about the meaning of what we have prayed. That is when the confession-making process begins.

Doctrine

When we state the meaning of a biblical idea we have created a doctrine. Doctrine comes from the Latin word *doctrina,* which means the content of what is taught. For Christians, a doctrine is the teaching of Scripture on a particular theme. For example, the doctrine of God would be the teaching of all things that the Bible says about God. That would be a pretty tall order, of course. So we tend to break down a vast topic like the doctrine of God into subtopics. Now let us return to our biblical phrase from the Lord's Prayer. Note how many subtopics about God are indicated in just those few words. God is ours, a father, and dwells in heaven. Clearly, each of those concepts needs explanation and further development by looking at all scriptural material that would shed light on it. As we do that we are developing doctrines—general concepts—derived from a synthesis of many biblical passages.

Dogma

Dogma and its adjective, dogmatic, tend to be unwelcome words in our contemporary vocabulary. We use them to refer to ideas and people who are, in our judgment, narrow, inflexible, and probably biased. In its Greek origin, the word expressed a pleasant idea, "that which seems good." In Greek philosophy, a dogma was an axiomatic principle which seemed settled forever. It referred to that which seemed so obviously good to everyone that no further discussion about it was needed.

Religiously, the word "dogma" was used to apply to a doctrine which had been formulated by some authoritative ecclesiastical body, like a church council, and which had been declared, by that body, to rest upon divine authority. For example, the first two ecumenical councils (so-called because they represented the whole household of God in the known world at that time) were the councils of Nicaea in A.D. 325 and Constantinople in A.D. 381. The Nicene Creed in our *Book of Confessions* was derived from statements of these two councils. It begins, "We believe in one God the Father Almighty, Maker of heaven and earth, and of all things visible and invisible." The simple prayer fragment "Our Father who art in heaven" has now been developed into a dogma, an official teaching of the ecumenical Christian church.

Dogmatics, or Systematic Theology

A further step in our process of thinking about biblical ideas can be the development of dogmatics, or systematic theology. Both terms evoke negative reaction in some quarters today. Originally they were simply meant to designate the orderly study of doctrines and dogmas in an attempt to state all that we may learn from Scripture. Theologians are those who speak *(legō)* about God *(theos).* As they do, they necessarily—and often helpfully—strive to systematize, synthesize, or organize all that we believe we have learned from Scripture into a meaningful whole. For example, traditionally, systematic theologians have discussed the doctrines of God, humankind, sin, salvation, church, and last things. In Europe, this activity has been called "dogmatics," probably because of the greater emphasis on the development of our doctrinal ideas from the dogmas formulated throughout history by the churches.

In the Anglo-Saxon world, the term "systematic theology" is now often associated with the post-Reformation effort to create a logical, comprehensive, and seemingly closed system of theological knowledge. Some theologians now prefer the term "constructive theology" to describe their discipline of clarifying religious ideas, even though they may find the possibility of a system offensive or out of reach. In an earlier era, Presbyterian ministers, when they were ordained, had to respond affirmatively to the question, "Do you sincerely receive and adopt the Confession of Faith and Catechisms of this Church, as containing the system of doctrine taught in the Scriptures?" As awareness grew that the Bible itself does not contain a system of thought but that we create a system from the biblical materials, candidates for ordination found that form of subscription unhelpful, and it was changed. The present form of subscription better expresses the various appropriate levels of commitment: "Will you be a minister of the Word in obedience to Jesus Christ, under the authority of Scripture, and continually guided by our confessions?" Elders and deacons take a similar vow.

Ecumenical Creeds

The word "creed" comes from the Latin *credo,* meaning "I believe." It indicates, first, an acknowledgment of personal trust in God. Note that the form is not "I believe that God exists." It is a statement of personal commitment, not mere ideas. "I believe in God" means that I entrust my life to this person, God. Second, a creed is a statement of the content of my personal commitment, a declaration not only that I believe but of what I believe. In this secondary sense, a creed is a concrete expression of personal experience. It is a way of handing on a tradition to the next generation. Here also the meaning behind the words is significant. The word "tradition" comes from the Latin *tradere,* which means both "to hand over" and "to betray." We live with that tension. There is always a danger when we hand over to others the statement of what we have believed. We may unintentionally betray or change, make artificial, or falsify what we have held dear. But we must take that risk. There is a greater danger in not handing on the tradition, in failing to witness to our faith, in refusing to share the good news God has given us.

Creeds developed in the early church in response to two different needs. The first need was for the instruction of new converts in the Christian faith. The church remembered the mandate of the Lord, "Go therefore and make disciples of all nations, baptizing them in the name of the Father and of the Son and the Holy Spirit, teaching them to observe all that I have commanded you" (Matt. 28:19–20). Converts to the faith were baptized in the name of the Father, Son, and Holy Spirit. At that time, these new members of the church were expected to make an affirmation of their faith in this Trinitarian God. For that to be meaningful, they first had to be instructed in the meaning of the faith they were to proclaim. The converts were therefore called "catechumens," those who were being instructed in the doctrines and discipline of the church they were entering, and their instruction was called "catechesis." They were usually asked questions and taught answers as a means of helping them understand and also remember this doctrinal teaching. Later manuals of Christian doctrine were prepared, in question-and-answer form, which were called "catechisms."

A second need of the early church was for authentic and authoritative statements of belief. There were false teachers whose ideas moved off at a tangent from the main stream of the church. Orthodoxy meant, literally, right opinion. Heresy meant, originally, to choose another way than that of the main body of Christians. Because of a proliferation of opinions, biblical interpretations, and independent teachings, the early church found it necessary to meet, to decide, and finally to declare what, in the judgment of the majority, was the truth of the gospel. Creeds were authoritative statements of belief. The Nicene Creed was the first such statement of the whole church in response to controversy. That is why it is placed first in our *Book of Confessions.* Creeds were also called "symbols," pointers toward the truth. In some places, the study of creeds is still called "symbolics." These early creeds were symbols of the unity of the visible church.

National Confessions

As the various European nations experienced Protestant Reformation in the sixteenth century, the leaders of the church in that nation would draw up a confession of their distinctive belief. The Augsburg Confession (1530) was the statement of Lutheran Germany. The Belgic Confession (1561) was the declaration of the church in the low countries, Belgium and the Netherlands. The Scots Confession (1560) marked Scotland's change from Roman Catholicism to Protestantism. The Heidelberg Catechism (1563) became the standard for the Palatinate region of Germany. And the Westminster Confession of Faith (1646) was designed to reform the doctrinal character of the Church of England.

These national confessions presupposed the ecumenical creeds and usually they explicitly announced their solidarity with the scriptural teaching of the creeds. Additionally, they stressed justification by grace through faith, which has been called the thirteenth article of the creed (following the traditional twelve articles of the Apostles' Creed). Confessions also criticized what were perceived to be the false views of the Roman Catholic Church on the one hand and, on the other, the sects of the Anabaptists, who rejected infant Baptism and opposed close ties between church and state. Protestant Reformers were trying to find a middle way. They contrasted themselves to the medieval establishment of Roman Catholicism, which they deemed corrupt in doctrine and morals. They also rejected the "radical reformation" of the Anabaptists, which in their opinion went too far in withdrawing from both church and society. Confessional bodies desired, normally, to be the national church of the land and to have their views adhered to by all citizens. The notion of the separation of church and state had not yet dawned. At the same time, the confessions did recognize an "invisible church," composed of all true believers and not limited by national boundaries.

The Modern Ecumenical Era

The age of classic confessions in Europe ended with the Westminster Confession of Faith, completed in 1646. That Presbyterian confession had a pervasive effect in the New World of the American colonies. In 1648, the Massachusetts Bay Colony adopted the Cambridge Platform, which embodied the Westminster Confession, modified to affirm the Congregational form of church government. In 1707, one year after Francis Makemie had gathered the first presbytery, the Philadelphia Baptist Association accepted the Philadelphia Confession of Faith. This document was the Westminster Confession of Faith, modified to mandate

Congregational polity and amended to affirm that only adult believers should be baptized.

A new situation arose in the eighteenth century. Empirical science began to set the standards for people's thought. There was significant reaction to the conflict and bitterness associated with confessional divisions. Attention shifted away from doctrinal refinements to the need for evangelism and missions. People reasoned that bringing the gospel to those who had not heard it in its simplicity was more important than clarifying the differences between competing Christian denominations. There was less interest in dogmatic pronouncements than in moral endeavor.

Historians have referred to America in the nineteenth century as a "benevolent empire." An enormous network of voluntary societies sprang up dedicated to spreading the gospel and transforming the culture. Students at Williams College in 1806 launched the modern foreign missionary movement. In 1810, the American Board of Commissioners for Foreign Missions was formed, with Presbyterians playing a leading role. Other voluntary societies designed to promote Christianity and morality included the American Bible Society (1816), the American Tract Society (1825), and the American Society for the Promotion of Temperance (1826). Most significant from the perspective of later history was the American Anti-Slavery Society (1833), which at its peak claimed a quarter of a million members. Preachers like Theodore D. Weld held revival meetings in which they preached to save people's souls and protested against the sin of slavery.

The American Civil War, with the issues of states' rights and slavery, shattered the Christian cultural consensus of the nineteenth century. In addition, during the next fifty years, Christians were increasingly divided as the Fundamentalist/Modernist controversy polarized people along doctrinal and ideological lines. In the 1930s many American churches split, over doctrine and other issues; with the

Depression, the cynicism which had gripped Europe after World War I finally came to America. Then came World War II, the holocaust in which six million Jews died, and science was used to create an atomic holocaust over Hiroshima. Doctrinal and denominational divisions no longer seemed so important. It was Christianity versus a growing secularism.

In 1948, the World Council of Churches, headquartered in Geneva, Switzerland, was formed with strong support from the Reformed and Presbyterian churches. The attention of leaders in mainline churches was centered on the modern ecumenical movement. American Presbyterians played leading roles, with Eugene Carson Blake, a former Stated Clerk of the General Assembly, becoming General Secretary in 1966.

Church Unity and Confessions

The ecumenical momentum toward unity began to have results, not only in organizations for interchurch cooperation but in mergers, reunions, and the creations of new union denominations. With these unions came a renewal of confessional activity as people sought to express the theological basis for their renewed life together. The United Church of Canada, a merger of Presbyterian, Congregational, and Methodist communions in 1924, included a doctrinal statement of 20 articles in the *Basis of Union.* The United Church of Christ, a merger of Congregational Christian Churches and the Evangelical and Reformed Church, issued a "Statement of Faith" in 1959. The World Council of Churches itself gave considerable attention to confessional matters, especially with the admission of the Eastern Orthodox Churches. The basis statement of the Council, since 1961, reads: "The World Council of Churches is a fellowship of churches which confess the Lord Jesus Christ as God and Saviour according to the

Scriptures and therefore seek to fulfill together their common calling to the glory of the one God, Father, Son, and Holy Spirit."

The Confession of 1967 of The United Presbyterian Church in the U.S.A. resulted in part from the 1958 merger of the Presbyterian Church in the U.S.A. with the United Presbyterian Church of North America. It was ecumenical in style and intent and was offered by the General Assembly to other churches. The request was made that this Presbyterian confession be studied and compared with Scripture and viewed as a possible basis for a union confession with other Christian bodies.

The Special Committee to Prepare a Brief Statement of the Reformed Faith, appointed after the reunion in 1983, comes out of a long-sought and much celebrated merger of Presbyterian churches, north and south. The Committee is very conscious of the mood and movement toward ecumenical unity. It is also acutely aware of the need for Presbyterians to clarify their common identity. It may be the first committee chosen to prepare a common confession of faith for which the attempt to represent pluralism within the church was a prerequisite. The mandate, followed by Moderator Taylor, was to represent "diversities of points of view and groups within the reunited church." Accordingly, the committee membership attempts to represent all people of the church and includes women and men, Black, Hispanic, and Asian, laypersons and clergy, theologians and people in other fields. Within that diversity, Moderator Taylor sought unity through four criteria which applied to everyone selected. All members, in his judgment, possessed (1) an authentic experience of faith, (2) experience in the life of the church, (3) training and ability in the disciplines of theology, and (4) capacity to articulate their own opinions and to be open to the opinions of others. This Committee will depend heavily on input from others, in the church and outside it. It is therefore crucial to the success of producing a new confession for the Presbyterian Church (U.S.A.) that members, and especially office-bearers, in the whole church be equally engaged in the task of understanding our Reformed heritage and relating it to the contemporary ecumenical setting.

The Book of Confessions, which we will now explore, contains two ancient creeds, the Nicene Creed and the Apostles' Creed. It encompasses four confessions, representing four different nations: the Scots Confession (Scotland), the Second Helvetic Confession (Switzerland), the Westminster Confession of Faith (England), and the Confession of 1967 (United States of America). There are three catechisms: the Heidelberg Catechism and the Westminster Larger and Shorter Catechisms. It also presents the Theological Declaration of Barmen. This declaration is a "clarification" (*Erklärung* in German) of the confessing churches of Germany against the threatening evil of Nazism. A plurality of confessional expressions has always been characteristic of the Reformed tradition. Our task will be to accent the common themes within these plural forms. Those themes forming the "essential tenets" of the Reformed faith give identity to our contemporary Presbyterian community. It is precisely those themes which will be our current contribution to the ecumenical movement, as we continue to learn from others of different traditions.

I

Ancient Creeds

3

The Nicene Creed
Fourth Century A.D.

The Nicene Creed was the first official doctrinal statement of the whole Christian church. It developed from the work of the first two ecumenical councils, Nicaea in 325 and Constantinople in 381, and was accepted as a definitive statement by the prestigious Council of Chalcedon in 451, after two centuries of struggle to clarify the relationship of Jesus Christ to God and to humanity. It has been used in worship ever since the sixth century as part of the communion service.

This creed, in its present form, is the oldest theological statement of the church, and it is the only creed accepted and used by all three major branches of Christendom: Eastern Orthodox, Roman Catholic, and Protestant. It is highly appropriate that it stands first in our Presbyterian (U.S.A.) *Book of Confessions*. It reminds us that the distinctive beliefs of the Reformed faith are those we hold in common with all Christians from the earliest times and to the present day. The deity and humanity of Jesus Christ and the personal reality of the Holy Spirit are primary among those catholic distinctives.

Historical Context: The Case of the Nicene Creed

On June 14, 325, the Emperor Constantine the Great entered the city of Nicaea in a stately procesession. Having only recently unified his empire militarily and politically,

Constantine had been troubled by divisions in the church over theological issues. In his mind, a unified empire demanded a unified church. "Disorder in the church," he said, "I consider more fearful than any other war." So under the guidance of what he regarded as a divine inspiration, he had summoned a universal council of the church to judge the controversy.

Constantine was joined by 318 bishops of the ecumenical church who would debate and decide the issues. Nicaea had been chosen because its name, "Victory," was a good omen, it had a pleasant climate, and it was only twenty miles from Constantine's imperial residence. The city had become jammed with tourists, merchants, beggars, and the religious faithful, all hoping to benefit from the presence of the council. Constantine hoped that the decisions reached there would resolve the theological division in the church and ensure peace in his empire.

Early Christian Teachers

As the Christian church spread and increased numerically, it became increasingly important to explain the faith to inquirers and to defend it against critics. Christians had not only to worship but also to think about the meaning of their faith.

The first Christian teacher to develop a systematic theology was Origen (d. c. A.D. 254). He interpreted the Bible using the concepts of Greek philosophy, especially the school of thought known as Neoplatonism. So sweeping was his scope and so pioneering his effort that later students of his thought were able to develop his insights in many different directions.

One of Origen's followers was Eusebius of Caesarea (d.c. A.D. 339). Eusebius compiled the first history of the church and became bishop of Caesarea. His history provided a defense of his churchmanship. He pointed to two historical foci: Jesus Christ, whose deeds testified to his divinity, and

Constantine the Great, who when he became emperor had ended persecution of the church and brought peace to the world.

Arius Challenges

Eusebius received into his diocese a young refugee priest named Arius. Arius asserted that he had had to flee Alexandria because the bishop of that city rejected the new philosophical theology and was intolerant of differing opinions. Arius had received his theological training under Lucian of Antioch, a student of Origen. From Lucian, Arius had learned Aristotle's philosophy. Like Lucian, Arius taught that Christ was subordinate to the Father. He defended belief in only one God as fundamental to the Christian faith, citing Deuteronomy 6:4. A logical conclusion was that the Son was not therefore of the same nature as the Father but was created out of nothing. Otherwise there would be two gods. Arius claimed biblical support for his views from Proverbs 8:22 and John 14:28.

On these grounds, Arius had come to oppose the bishop of his diocese, Alexander. The bishop, he argued, was advocating views akin to those of the heretics Sabellius and Paul of Samosata. (Sabellius spoke of God as a Monad, a single unit; Father, Son, and Spirit were, for him, just three ways in which the one God is manifested to the world. Paul of Samosata had been condemned at Antioch in A.D. 268 for teaching that Christ was of one substance—*homoousios* in Greek—with the Father.) Arius accordingly wrote to Alexander to explain his position: that there is only one God, and the Son or Word (*Logos* in Greek) was "of another substance" than the Father. Arius wrote in a similar vein to a former fellow student of Lucian, Bishop Eusebius of Nicomedia, who warmly supported him. As for those who disagreed with him, Arius described them heretics or "unlearned men."

Bishop Alexander Replies

Bishop Alexander of Alexandria defended his position in a letter to all the bishops of the church. He criticized Eusebius of Nicomedia and condemned Arius as a propounder of heresies. Alexander was particularly disturbed by the implication that the Son could change. He wrote, "How can he be mutable and susceptible of change, who says of himself, 'I am in the Father, and the Father in me'; and 'I and the Father are one'; and again by the Prophet, 'Behold me because I am, and have not changed'?"

Hosius of Cordova Tries to Negotiate

Nearly two years before the council, Constantine had attempted to negotiate a settlement between the major parties. He dispatched a letter to Alexandria addressed to both Bishop Alexander and Arius, expressing his impatience with what he considered a needless and senseless dispute. The emperor urged that both parties stop the controversy, because otherwise the people might be led into "blasphemy or schism."

The letter was brought to Alexandria and interpreted by Bishop Hosius of Cordova, Constantine's theological adviser. Hosius himself was steeped in the western antiphilosophical tradition of the Latin theologian Tertullian (c. A.D. 160–230), whose slogan was, "What has Jerusalem to do with Athens, the Church with the Academy?" Hosius returned to Rome with a report of no progress in his discussions with Alexander and Arius.

Further reports from the east told of increased strife in the church and even rioting in the streets between supporters of rival factions. Arius was reported to have a large lay following. Popular attention had been captured for Arius's view through the use of a poem set to the tune of a bawdy song well known in the taverns:

Arius of Alexandria, I'm the talk of all the town,
Friend of saints, elect of heaven, filled with learning
  and renown;
If you want the Logos-doctrine, I can serve it hot
  and hot:
God begat him and before he was begotten, He was not.

The Council Gathers

Such was the state of turbulence as the assembly met at Nicaea to debate the issues. Together with the bishops, there were many presbyters and deacons in the church of St. Mary awaiting the arrival of the emperor. Many were scarred from the times of persecution: one with an eye put out; another who had been tortured with a red-hot iron. There were ascetics who had spent years as hermits in forests and caves. Eusebius of Caesarea, the historian, was present. So were the principals in the conflict: Arius was in the company of his advocate, Eusebius of Nicomedia; Alexander of Alexandria was accompanied by his theological adviser, Athanasius.

The moment the approach of the emperor was announced, all rose from their seats. "The emperor," Eusebius later wrote, "appeared like a heavenly messenger of God, covered with gold and gems, a glorious presence, very tall and slender, full of beauty, strength, and majesty." Constantine in his opening speech called on the assembly to put away all causes of strife and prayed that the Holy Spirit might guide their counsels to a right and harmonious issue.

It soon became plain that there were three main groups or parties. The views of Arius were defended by about twenty bishops, led by Eusebius of Nicomedia. At the other extreme were the followers of Alexander, also a minority group. Their adviser was Athanasius, and they stood firm on the declaration that Jesus was of one substance with the Father. The spokesman and leader of the vast majority seemed to be Eusebius of Caesarea, who continually sought the middle ground.

Athanasius Argues

Athanasius attempted to free his hearers from thinking of God in terms of nature or philosophy. "God is not nature," he said, "nor is he the totality of its parts." God, he said, is rather both the source of being (Creator) and the order of the universe (Word). Athanasius condemned Arianism as a form of philosophical thinking in the guise of Christian theology. Theology, Athanasius argued, was based on God's revelation in Scripture and dealt with human salvation. The issue was salvation. "If the Son were a creature, man had remained mortal as before; for a creature had not joined creatures to God." Salvation would not have been possible had the Word been (as Arius taught) a part of creation, "for with a creature, the devil, himself a creature, would have ever continued the battle."

Constantine Intervenes

Constantine followed the debates with interest. Proposals and counterproposals were offered to clarify the issues. Then Constantine called on Eusebius of Caesarea to suggest a formula that might be accepted as a compromise. Eusebius offered a creedal statement used in his own diocese, which read:

> We believe in one God, the Father almighty, maker of all things visible and invisible.
>
> And in one Lord Jesus Christ, the Logos of God, God from God, light from light, life of life, Son only-begotten, first-begotten of all creation, begotten before all the ages from the Father, through Whom also all things came into being, Who because of our salvation was incarnate and dwelt among men, and suffered, and rose again on

the third day, and ascended to the Father, and will come again in glory to judge living and dead;

We believe also in one Holy Spirit.

As the statement was read, Constantine listened attentively and approved it warmly. The bishops also responded favorably. Phrases such as "according to tradition" and "scriptural" were heard throughout the church.

The minority party that followed Alexander proved unyielding in its opposition, however. The formula proposed by Eusebius of Caesarea did not deal with the problem as they saw it. Not even Arius denied that the Son was God, and the phrase "God from God" was quite acceptable to the Arians. Since, the Arians argued, all things are from God, there could be no objection to saying that the Son is from God. So the minority who supported Alexander pushed the assembly to a clearer and more precise definition.

Various amendments were proposed as the debate proceeded. One bishop suggested that the Son should be defined as "the true power and image of the Father." Others supported the phrase "in all things exactly like the Father." Winking and whispering advice to each other, the Arians accepted the amendments with no hesitation.

Only the Alexandrians were not satisfied. Constantine knew that there would be no peace unless they gave their assent. Some term was needed which defined the Son and the Father as of the *same* substance. Constantine determined to propose it himself, hoping by his influence to balance the forces and arrive at a stable settlement. The emperor rose. The relation of the Son to the Father, he announced, would best be expressed by the term *homoousios*.

The assembly was at once in turmoil, but after an initial flurry of excitement, the bishops at Nicaea quickly accepted the emperor Constantine's proposal. They accepted an amended creed which declared that Jesus Christ, the Son of God, was "begotten not made, being of one substance *(homoousios)* with the Father." Only two bishops continued to defend Arius's views, and with Arius they were excommunicated and deprived of their positions. All the others eventually subscribed to the formula.

Constantine himself viewed the creed as a final and inspired statement of truth. He was confident that it would bring peace and unity to the church and to the empire.

Nicene Orthodoxy Declines

However, some of the bishops at Nicaea had subscribed to the *homoousios* formula only in deference to the emperor—or, at least, on the assumption that a broad interpretation was permissible. Arianism was not defeated but merely driven underground. Deep-seated theological divisions were sharpened by the fact that the emperor had forced the decision at the council and was enforcing it in his empire.

In the east, Arianism came to prevail. Constantine's son, Constantius, embraced the views of the excommunicated presbyter with a passion. Arius himself was readmitted to communion two years after the council. Eusebius of Nicomedia, the staunch defender of Arian views at Nicaea, was elected bishop of Constantinople. Athanasius, who succeeded Alexander as bishop of Alexandria, suffered banishment no fewer than five times. One of the periods of exile was a punishment for refusing to readmit Arius to the Alexandrian church.

From 350 to 361, Constantius controlled the empire. He set about opposing Nicene orthodoxy with vigor. The Arians surfaced and, with the emperor's backing, succeeded in gaining wide approval for their beliefs at a series of councils.

The rising strength of Arian extremism brought the moderate majority in the church together again in order to deal with the internal dissension. At a meeting in Sirmium, called by the emperor Contantius in 358, they proposed the inclusive term *homoiousios,* saying of the Son, "God like to the Father who begat him according to the Scriptures." The words *homoousios* and *homoiousios* differed in spelling by only one letter. The difference in meaning was that the first meant "same" substance and the second meant "like" or "similar" substance. Athanasius returned from exile and, for the sake of unity within the church, threw his support behind this second, compromise word.

The Problem of Apollinarius of Laodicea

During this period a marked shift in the Christological controversy took place when Bishop Apollinarius of Laodicea (c. A.D. 310–390) began to apply the results of Nicaea to the question of Jesus' human nature. The bishop was a friend and co-worker of Athanasius and a strong supporter of the *homoousion* theology.

Theologically, Apollinarius wrestled with the question of Christ's soul (or mind) and spirit. Philosophically, he struggled with the problem of how two essences could be combined into one. The flesh of Jesus, he contended, was joined in absolute oneness of being with the Godhead from the moment of conception.

For Apollinarius this meant that the divine Word, or Logos, took the place of Christ's mind, will, and energy. The advantages of this view, he taught, were that it excluded the possibility of contradictory wills or sinful thoughts or physical passions in Christ. For Apollinarius, Christ was unchangeable.

Opposition to Apollinarius

A group of three theologians known as the Cappadocian Fathers (Basil the Great, Gregory of Nyssa, and Gregory Nazianzus) led the opposition to Apollinarius. Even they proceeded with reluctance because of the brilliance of his arguments and the personal respect in which he was widely held.

Athanasius was also forced to join them in the fight against his old friend. He noted that, in Apollinarius's teaching, Christ was not a real human being but only "appeared as a human." The church, Athanasius had argued, could not accept such a "docetic," apparent, or sham incarnation. Christ had a human soul and spirit. He wept, he was anguished, he prayed. Athanasius contended that removing a normal human psychology from Christ clashed with the biblical picture of a Savior who developed, who was limited in knowledge, who suffered and underwent every kind of human experience.

The Council of Constantinople, A.D. 381

In 380 a new Emperor, Theodosius I, issued an edict requiring his subjects to profess the "orthodox" faith of Nicaea. He raised Gregory Nazianzus to the patriarchal throne of Constantinople. Finally, he called a second ecumenical council to assemble in Constantinople in May 381.

The resurgent Arians, the Nicene orthodox who supported Athanasius, the moderate *homoiousians,* and the adherents of Apollinarius came together. Like Constantine before him, the new emperor attended the sessions and showed favor to the venerable bishops. The Christian historian Socrates Scholasticus (c. A.D. 380–450) gave a vivid picture of the failure of the differing sides to understand one another at the council: "The situation was exactly like a battle at night, for both parties seemed to be in the dark about the grounds on which they were hurling abuse at each other." The council framed no new creed or symbol, but the 150 bishops agreed to a modification of the Nicaean formula which became known as the Nicene Creed.

> We believe in one God, the Father Almighty, Maker of heaven and earth, and of all things visible and invisible;

And in one Lord Jesus Christ, the only-begotten Son of God, begotten of the Father before all worlds, God of God, Light of Light, Very God of Very God, begotten, not made, being of one substance with the Father; by whom all things were made; who for us men, and for our salvation, came down from heaven, and was incarnate by the Holy Spirit of the Virgin Mary, and was made man, and was crucified also for us under Pontius Pilate. He suffered and was buried, and the third day he rose again according to the Scriptures, and ascended into heaven, and sitteth on the right hand of the Father. And he shall come again with glory to judge both the quick and the dead, whose kingdom shall have no end.

And we believe in the Holy Spirit, the Lord and Giver of Life, who proceedeth from the Father, who with the Father and the Son together is worshipped and glorified, who spoke by the prophets. And we believe one holy catholic and apostolic Church. We acknowledge one baptism for the remission of sins. And we look for the resurrection of the dead, and the life of the world to come. Amen.

Essential Tenets of the Reformed Faith

The Person of Jesus Christ

Jesus Christ is the center of the Christian faith. The Nicene Creed expresses the church's understanding of what Scripture teaches about who Jesus Christ is. The question is Jesus' relationship to God and to us as humans. What is at stake, as Athanasius said, is our salvation: How may we as humans be related to God? The church struggled for two hundred years and through four ecumenical councils to come to a satisfactory answer. That answer, once given, retained the consent of all Christian bodies for over 1500 years.

Some have joked that the Christological councils were

squabbling over an *iota,* the smallest letter in the Greek alphabet. For Greek-speaking bishops, the difference, in part, lay between *homoousios* and *homoiousios.* Was Jesus of the "same" substance with the Father or only of "like" or "similar" substance? Neither for the bishops of the second century nor for Presbyterians in the twentieth century is the issue unimportant. The issue is salvation. If God actually came in the flesh of a human being and if that God/person lived, suffered, died, and rose again for our sakes, then we can be united to God. So the church has affirmed. The hows and whys of the salvation process were debated and declared in later confessions. The Nicene Creed answers the first question: Is Jesus both divine and human? The answer is yes! The eternal Word of God is incarnate in Jesus Christ.

The Nicene Creed was not finally and officially accepted as the creed of the whole church until the Council of Chalcedon in 451. The council concluded the lengthy and elaborate debate on the person of Christ. It attempted through four terms or phrases to show the false tangents which the church should avoid and thus to mark off the center of the church's affirmation.

Each of the four Christological councils contributed one element to the final understanding. The Council of Nicaea, against Arius, affirmed that Jesus Christ was truly divine. The Council of Constantinople, against Apollinarius, affirmed that Jesus Christ was truly human. The Council of Ephesus, against Nestorius, affirmed that Jesus Christ was one integrated person. The Council of Chalcedon, against Eutyches, affirmed that Jesus Christ had two natures, divine and human.

Having said that Jesus Christ is divine and human, one person with two natures, does not mean that we fully understand our Savior. The person of Christ remains a mystery. We cannot fully understand Jesus Christ because he is unique. We have no adequate analogy with which to compare him. What the church has done is to protect the mystery. It has said that if we move off at a tangent in any one of four ways, denying the deity, humanity, one person, or two natures, we will have distorted the truth of the biblical witness regarding who Christ is. And, more important, the church has declared that this mystery of God becoming human in Christ is central to the mystery of our becoming one with God. A central comfort and assurance of the Christian faith is found in Jesus' words in John 14:19: "Because I live, you will live also."

The Reality of the Holy Spirit

The Nicene Creed also affirms the deity of the Holy Spirit and the unity of the Spirit with the Father and the Son. Just as it took time and effort to clarify the person of Christ, so there was development in the understanding of the person and relationship of the Holy Spirit. The statement adopted by the bishops at the Council of Nicaea ended with the simple phrase, "We believe also in one Holy Spirit." A half century later, the bishops at the Council of Constantinople added a paragraph explaining their understanding of the Holy Spirit. The Spirit is identified as Lord and life-giver, who spoke through the prophets. The Spirit is to be worshipped and glorified with the Father and the Son.

A source of controversy and division within the Christian church is an addition to the Nicene Creed made in the Middle Ages. The original form of the creed said of the Holy Spirit, "who proceedeth from the Father." In the Western church, between the seventh and eleventh centuries, many began to add the phrase "and the Son" (*filioque* in Latin). They were following the fifth-century theologian Augustine, who thought of the Spirit as the bond of love between the Father and the Son. Saying that the Spirit "proceedeth from the Father and the Son" may, to them, have been a way of reinforcing the deity of Christ. It also pointed to the New Testament teaching that the Spirit is the Spirit of Christ.

The Eastern church was incensed when a Western pope, Benedict VIII, officially added the phrase "and the Son" to the Nicene Creed in 1014. It appeared to them that this bishop of Rome was arrogating to himself a higher authority than an ecumenical council. The Eastern view located the unity of the Trinity in the Father, who begat the Son and generated the Spirit. The addition of *filioque* seemed to them also to demean the equality of the Spirit in the Trinity. And they could, with good cause, note that the phrase "and the Son" is not found in the key biblical text, John 15:26.

The Eastern Orthodox Church divided from what is now called the Roman Catholic Church in 1054. Disagreement over *filioque* was one of the occasions for this tragic split, which still continues. The Eastern Orthodox became full working partners with Protestants in the World Council of Churches, despite the fact that Protestants retained the phrase "and the Son."

Recently, a further step was taken toward healing the centuries-old East-West division. In Lima, Peru, in 1982, the Faith and Order Commission of the World Council of Churches called on the churches to recognize the Niceno-Constantinopolitan Creed as a fundamental confession of the ecumenical church. To make this possible, Protestant and Roman Catholic theologians and church leaders agreed to use the most ancient form of the creed without the *filioque* clause.

We are slowly learning to know and value emphases of the East in theology and worship which have long been obscure to us. The Eastern emphasis on the reality and presence of the Holy Spirit in worship and life can add a wholesome balance to Protestantism insofar as it has emphasized Christ alone. Despite past disagreements over *filioque*, the Nicene Creed has been and remains the one symbol of theological unity among all Christian churches.

Contemporary Relevance

Controversy Over Christological Language and Content

In recent years, Presbyterians have experienced significant controversy, and even division, over the central Nicene affirmation of the deity and humanity of Jesus Christ. Entangled in these debates of the late 1970s and early 1980s has been the issue of the nature of theological language. The Kaseman case in National Capitol Union Presbytery of the former United Presbyterian Church in the U.S.A. illustrates our confusion here.

Mansfield Kaseman, coming to the United Presbyterian Church from the United Church of Christ, defended his freedom to use nontraditional language to express what he believed about the person of Jesus Christ. For him it was of critical importance that the church be relevant to contemporary society by using the language of today. Others in his presbytery argued that Kaseman's language expressed a different view of who Christ is from that of the church. For Kaseman's accusers it was of critical importance that the church not change or obscure its commitment to the deity and humanity of Christ as affirmed in the Nicene Creed in our *Book of Confessions.* After two lengthy examinations on the floor of presbytery, two hearings before the Synod of the Piedmont, and two trials by the Permanent Judicial Commission of the former United Presbyterian Church in the U.S.A., the latter body ruled that Kaseman was orthodox. The Permanent Judicial Commission indicated that Kaseman's "answers to some questions may appear to be weak, or less than wholly adequate." However, "when all answers are considered in the context of the complete transcript of the examination, the record shows that the Presbytery acted reasonably, responsibly, and deliberately within the Constitution of the Church." The Permanent Judicial Commission therefore concluded that what Kaseman intended to say was what the church affirms. The Permanent Judicial Commission reaffirmed the biblical and confessional position as traditionally stated by the church.

> The doctrines of the Church identified in the appellant's specifications of error, including the Trinity, the Person of Jesus Christ as Son of God and second Person of the Trinity, the Atonement and Saving Death of Jesus Christ, and the Bible as the Word of God, are not at issue here so far as the Church and its confessional stance are concerned. These doctrines are clearly set forth in the Book of Confessions. The Church has included them in its faith and continues to affirm them, including the full deity and full humanity of Jesus Christ in a full confessional context.

The General Assembly of the United Presbyterian Church in 1981 also strongly asserted the denomination's commitment to the full deity and humanity in the one person of Jesus Christ.

We can learn from our study of the Nicene Creed that the final issue is never language alone but rather the essential meaning that our language is meant to convey. Part of what took two hundred years for the early church to unravel was differences in the use of words. In the fourth century, during the Council of Nicaea, the dominant philosophies of the day identified ultimate reality by the words "substance" or "essence." In Stoic philosophy the word was *hypostasis,* while in Platonic thought it was *ousia.* These Greek words translated into Latin as *substantia* (substance). If ultimate reality was a substance, then Jesus Christ could be either a divine substance or a human substance, but he could not be both, or so the philosophers contended.

By the end of the period of the Christological councils, a significant shift in philosophical thought and language had taken place. Now, not *substantia* (substance) but *prosopon* (person) was used to symbolize ultimate reality. At that point it was possible for philosophers, as well as people of faith, to conceive of Jesus Christ as having two natures (substances) in one person. The reality was the person of Jesus Christ.

One lesson we may learn from the experience of the early church is to fasten on the meaning of words, on their content, and not to absolutize any one form of words. The purpose of studying the Nicene Creed is not to force everyone to use the ancient philosophical language of "same substance." We should use whatever contemporary language will best express to people the central truth. In simplest terms, the Nicene Creed says: Whatever God is, Jesus is that; and whatever humanity is, Jesus is that too, in one whole person.

Controversy Over the Charismatic Movement

The stress in the Nicene Creed on the reality of the Holy Spirit is also instructive for us today. In the last two decades, mainline churches, including the Presbyterian Church, have seen a reawakening of interest in the person and work of the Holy Spirit. The modern Charismatic movement, in one sense, can be dated from 1960, when a renewed experience of the Holy Spirit by Dennis Bennett, an Episcopal priest in California, received national publicity. Since then thousands of Christians, including Presbyterians, have used the language of "baptism in the Spirit" to express a renewing and vital experience with God. Because this new experience has sometimes included such phenomena as speaking in tongues, it has on occasion led to controversy in Presbyterian churches. There has been a judicial case, and there are important study documents which have advised a cautious and open attitude on the part of all Presbyterians to various forms of experience of the Holy Spirit.

Protestants are descendants of the Western church. When the Eastern Orthodox Church split off in the eleventh century, we lost touch with some of the vital interest in and experience of the Holy Spirit in our life and worship. There have always been undercurrents of mysticism in Western Christianity, both Catholic and Protestant. But the main body has felt more comfortable with thought than with experience. Now that imbalance is being challenged, in one form, by the contemporary Charismatic movement. As Presbyterians, we need to be discerning about the Spirit's work based on our study of Scripture and our understanding of the Reformed tradition. Careful studies of both the person and work of the Holy Spirit resulted in major reports to the United Presbyterian Church in 1970 and to the Presbyterian Church in the U.S. in 1971.

For Presbyterians, Spirit and Word are never separable. Not every claim to an experience of the Spirit need be accepted uncritically. At the same time, we Western, Protestant, Presbyterian Christians can conceivably learn something new in the realm of the experience of the Spirit. In May 1966, a group of loyal Presbyterians organized the Presbyterian Charismatic Communion. It became a means of communication and cooperation for Presbyterian and Reformed pastors and laypersons involved in the charismatic renewal movement. In 1984 the name of the organization was changed to Presbyterian and Reformed Renewal Ministries International, reflecting the inclusion in the body of representatives from twenty-six Presbyterian and Reformed denominations. Members of this group are eager to share what for them has been a renewing experience of the Holy Spirit, whom the Nicene Creed says is to be worshipped and glorified with the Father and the Son.

4

The Apostles' Creed
Second to Ninth Centuries A.D.

The Apostles' Creed is the most widely used confessional statement in the Western church. It is by far the best known among laypersons. Most Christian people have memorized the Apostles' Creed along with the Lord's Prayer. It is used in worship more often than any other creedal formula.

The three ecumenical creeds, the Nicene, the Athanasian (now little known), and the Apostles', provided a link between the Protestant Reformation and the early church. By affirming the biblical character of the teachings of the ecumenical creeds, the Reformers sought to establish continuity with the earliest Christians and show that it was the medieval church which had departed from the early Christian standard. Luther expounded the Apostles' Creed in the second chapter of his Small Catechism, which set the pattern for most Reformation doctrinal expositions. From the simple and brief Small Catechism of Luther to the complex and continually expanded *Institutes of the Christian Religion* by John Calvin, the basic structure was an explanation of the Apostles' Creed, the Lord's Prayer, and the Ten Commandments.

Next to the Nicene Creed, the Apostles' Creed is the most universally accepted doctrinal statement in Christendom. It grew from a baptismal formula and is now often incorporated in the liturgy of regular Sunday services. In the modern era, as early as 1927 at a World Conference on Faith and Order, church leaders from East and West joined in reciting it and in accrediting it as a fitting expression of the Christian message.

Historical Context: The Case of the Apostles' Creed

Garibaldus, Bishop of Le Liège, in southern France, sat staring at a letter from the Holy Roman Emperor, Charlemagne (Charles the Great). The ninth century A.D. had just begun, and the emperor was concerned that there be uniformity in the teaching given by all priests in his kingdom. To that end, he insisted that people were not qualified to be godparents unless they knew by heart and could repeat the Apostles' Creed. Indeed, the emperor believed that all Christians should know the Lord's Prayer and the Apostles' Creed and be able to teach them to others. Certainly all priests should know and be able to explain these basic Christian documents. Bishop Garibaldus began to compose his reply, assuring the emperor that in his diocese all priests knew and used the Apostles' Creed, which had been in a fixed form for many years.

Biblical Origins

The beginnings of creeds are found in the Bible. In Deuteronomy, in the Old Testament, there are several forms by which the people of Israel remembered God's mighty acts of deliverance and repeated them to their children. Perhaps the most well known and most creedlike is found in Deuteronomy 6:4–5: "Hear, O Israel: The LORD our God is one LORD; and you shall love the LORD your God with all your heart, and with all your soul, and with all your might."

A precursor among ancient Hebrews of the catechism style of teaching was a story form of recital such as that in Deuteronomy 26:5–9:

> And you shall make response before the LORD your God, "A wandering Aramean was my father; and he went down into Egypt and sojourned there, few in number; and there he became a nation, great, mighty, and populous. And the Egyptians treated us harshly, and afflicted us, and laid upon us hard bondage. Then we cried to the LORD the God of our fathers, and the LORD heard our voice, and saw our affliction, our toil, and our oppression; and the LORD brought us out of Egypt with a mighty hand and an outstretched arm, with great terror, with signs and wonders; and he brought us into this place and gave us this land, a land flowing with milk and honey."

No creeds, confessions, or catechisms in the formal sense are found in the New Testament, except perhaps for the briefest but most central statement of all, "Jesus is Lord." What is manifest is a common body of doctrine, accepted by all as the confession of the church as a whole.

Fragments of creeds are found throughout the New Testament. There are many possible pointers to the more fully developed faith of the church. Jesus asked his disciples, "Who do people say the Son of man is?" Simon Peter replied for his comrades, "You are the Messiah, the Son of the Living God" (Matt. 16:13, 16 TEV). The apostle Paul declared that every tongue should "confess that Jesus Christ is Lord" (Phil. 2:11). To the Corinthians, Paul proclaimed, "For I delivered to you as of first importance what I also received, that Christ died for our sins in accordance with the scriptures" (1 Cor. 15:3). To the Romans, Paul gave the exhortation, "If you confess with your lips that Jesus is Lord and believe in your heart that God raised him from the dead, you will be saved" (Rom. 10:9). To the Corinthians, Paul explained that "no one can say 'Jesus is Lord' except by the Holy Spirit" (1 Cor. 12:3). In contrast to the nineteenth-century theological view of Paul as an innovator of Christian doctrine, it would appear that he was careful to receive and transmit the body of teaching authoritatively held and handed on by the church.

The Rule of Faith

As early as the second half of the second century, Christians seemed to take for granted a summary of Christian doctrine called "the rule of faith." This was not the Apostles' Creed in its later, more developed form. It was, however, in various forms, an outline, a summary, a compendium of Christian teaching, embodying the teaching of the apostles and useful for training new Christians.

One reason we know so little about these early creedal statements was that Christians feared misunderstanding and persecution. There was what has been called the *disciplina arcani,* or rule of secrecy. For several centuries the central mysteries of the church, particularly Baptism and the Lord's Supper, were hidden from the uninitiated. Creedal statements were closely connected to these two sacraments, so no formal creeds were written down. The bishop (presbyter, elder, or pastor) delivered doctrinal formulas to candidates for Baptism, who memorized them and then recited them to the congregation when they were received into the church.

During the second and third centuries there was gradual development toward a more fixed form of creedal expression. In the mid-second century, Justin Martyr, a Christian Apologist—one who argued publicly for the truth of the Christian faith—was fond of quoting from semiformal creeds to show the unanimity of Christian teaching. Irenaeus, a Christian theologian in the second half of the second century, made the constant claim that the faith of the church was everywhere one and the same, a consensus he designated "the canon of truth." Tertullian, the first theologian to write in Latin, repeatedly appealed to a "rule of faith," a summary of biblical truth passed on by tradition. Hippolytus was a Roman contemporary of Tertullian at the end of the second and beginning of the third century; his *Apostolic Tradition* was the first document to show an apparently fixed creed. And in the late thirties of the third century, Origen, writing at Caesarea, referred to certain articles as being absolutely essential in what appeared to be a formal creed. Into the third century there were many creeds, reflecting a common body of orthodox belief, but no one fixed formula was recognized by all.

The Baptismal Setting

The sacrament of Baptism was the context from which the creed further developed. The personal tone with which the Apostles' Creed begins has its roots in the convert's being asked, "Do you believe in God the Father Almighty?" The person would answer "I believe" and then be baptized. This question-and-answer pattern would continue with affirmations of belief in Jesus Christ and the Holy Spirit. The threefold confession and threefold baptism were considered to wipe out the sins of one's former life.

Candidates for Baptism were taught the meaning of the solemn vows they were taking. It became customary at the end of the training period for the initiates to recite a creed that embodied the doctrine they were now going to profess.

Reciting a creed in this setting was understood as taking a solemn oath; indeed, the taking of an oath was the original meaning of the word "sacrament." Clement of Alexandria called the creed a "profession." Origen said it was an "agreement with God." The most common name for this creed recited at baptism was "symbol." The primary idea of a symbol in both Latin and Greek was that of a sign or token. The symbol reminded someone of something else. The recital of the creed reminded Christians of their baptism and their vow of trust in God the Father, Son, and Holy Spirit made when they were baptized.

The Old Roman Symbol

The first local creed to take definitive shape and then be used more widely was the Old Roman Symbol. Formed sometime in the latter part of the second century, it was apparently an enlargement of the simple Trinitarian confession widely used at baptism. And that formula itself pointed back to the biblical statement in Matthew 28:19–20, where Jesus commanded his followers, "Go therefore and make disciples of all nations, baptizing them in the name of the Father and of the Son and of the Holy Spirit, teaching them to observe all that I have commanded you." Most other creeds in the West descended from this Old Roman Symbol. The Apostles' Creed, too, was a descendant of the Roman creed, enriched with doctrine that had become important in the provinces.

The Legend of Apostolic Authorship

The title Apostles' Creed *(symbolum apostolorum)* first occurred in a letter sent by the Synod of Milan in 390 to Pope Siricius. It was probably drafted by Ambrose, Bishop of Milan. Ambrose was confident that the creed had been composed by the twelve apostles, who met, conferred, and each contributed a clause. This popular view of its origin was expressed by Rufinus, who in 404 wrote an exposition of the creed. He noted that the apostles had been equipped at Pentecost to speak different languages and were being sent out to preach the gospel in different lands. Rufinus wrote:

> As they were therefore on the point of taking leave of each other, they first settled an agreed norm for their future preaching, so that they might not find themselves, widely separated as they would be, giving out different doctrines to the people they invited to believe in Christ. So they met together in one spot and, being filled with

> the Holy Spirit, compiled this brief token, as I have said, of their future preaching, each making the contribution he thought fit; and they decreed that it should be handed out as standard teaching to believers.

Rufinus did not originate this story, he merely quotes it as one widely accepted in the latter half of the fourth century. The legend was elaborated in a series of sermons, entitled *The Symbol,* falsely attributed to Augustine. In the first of these sermons a particular phrase from the creed was attributed to each of the twelve apostles.

The legend was universally believed during the Middle Ages. It was first questioned at the Council of Florence (1438–1445), which attempted a reconciliation between churches in the East and West. When the Latin representatives cited the Apostles' Creed, the Greeks from the East exclaimed, "We do not possess and have never seen this creed of the apostles!" A Renaissance scholar, Lorenzo Valla, disproved the apostolic origin of the document. He was joined by an English bishop, Reginald Pecock, who denied apostolic authorship to the creed. So powerful was commitment to the legend, however, that Valla was forced to recant and Pecock had to resign his bishopric in 1458. At the time of the Protestant Reformation, the theory of direct apostolic authorship of the Apostles' Creed was quietly set aside by most scholars. The Reformers continued to accept the creed, however, as reflecting genuine apostolic teaching based on Scripture.

Formation in Southern France

The first literary witness to the form of the Apostles' Creed as we have it today was a Benedictine monk, Priminius, who came from southern France to Germany in the late eighth century. Priminius had not had an easy life. He was originally a native of Spain in the Pyrenees region. In 718, the Saracens fell on that area and devastated it.

Churches and their clergy were special objects of persecution. Priminius was forced to flee for his life before the onslaught. He came to know a form of the Apostles' Creed in southern France, in the area of Provence, which had been in use there since the fifth century.

Priminius went as a missionary to an area of southern Germany noted for the barbarism of its people. Liturgical, sacramental, and doctrinal standards were deplorable. He founded a monastery at Reichenau, near Lake Constance, where he wrote a missionary manual, a compendious handbook of Christian doctrine compiled from Scripture and authoritative tradition. This book was designed to equip him and his followers for their missionary efforts. Central to this text and cited in three separate contexts was the Apostles' Creed as we now have it. In one instance, Priminius recalled his readers to the solemn scene of their own baptism. He wrote:

> Thus we recall to your memories, brothers, the pact we made with God in the baptistery itself: that is, how, when we were severally asked by the priest our names and how we were called, either you yourself answered, if you were already of an age to answer, or at all events he who was undertaking the vow for you and lifted you up from the water answered.

Then followed the Apostles' Creed in question-and-response form between the priest and the new church member.

Authorization by the Emperor

Charlemagne united most of the Christian lands in what is now northern Europe into one superstate, the only medieval ruler to do so. In 800, he assumed the title of Holy Roman Emperor. During his reign he strove not only for political unity but for a cultural renewal, which became known as the Carolingian renaissance. As part of this cultural restoration, Charlemagne wanted to raise the educational level of priests and to institute standard forms of worship. The form of the Apostles' Creed known in France and Germany was, for him, an important aid in this endeavor. It became the test of a priest's grasp of the essentials of Christian teaching. Real knowledge of the gospel and not just rote memory was the goal; those who did not know Latin were allowed to learn the creed in their native French or German.

The letter Bishop Garibaldus of Le Liège received was but one among many actions the emperor took to ensure that the faithful were properly instructed, using the Apostles' Creed. In 811–813, he wrote to all church leaders in his realm, seeking detailed information on liturgical practices and specifically asking if they were using the creed. A council held at his direction in 813 sanctioned this ideal of doctrinal and liturgical uniformity.

By the opening of the ninth century, the received text of the Apostles' Creed, as we have it, exercised a virtual monopoly in Western Europe. In the ninth century, the Roman papacy, which Charlemagne had supported, took into the Roman liturgy the form of the creed used in Germany and France. Rome thereby received back, in enriched form, the same rule of faith it had known and helped develop from the second century on. Although the form had evolved slowly, the content was still the essential tenets of the gospel which Christians had known and taught since the days of the apostles.

Essential Tenets of the Reformed Faith

One God in Three Persons

The Apostles' Creed simply states the essential facts of the biblical message. It does not elucidate, elaborate, or explain. The focus is on God's person and God's personal activity in human history.

One God. The first fact is that God is one. That is the essential teaching of both the Old and the New Testaments, of Judaism and Christianity. The Christian doctrine of the Trinity is a way of reasserting monotheism, that God is one. The mystery of the Trinity asserts that Father, Son, and Spirit are each persons. But they are the personal manifestations of one God, not three gods. Our problem is having intellectual categories in which to make sense of this unique fact. It was only possible for early Christians to understand that Jesus Christ had two natures in one person when they could think of person, not nature, as the fundamental category of reality. To come to terms with the Trinity, we must think of God as the ultimate reality and of persons as receiving their reality from God. That does not mean that we will understand the Trinity. Christians for centuries have devised analogies and illustrations to try to make the Trinity understandable in their culture. The important commitment for us is to hold to the essentials of the biblical witness and not distort the facts in an attempt to make them understandable in our culture's conceptual categories.

Father. The second fact is that God is Father. For Christians today this raises an immediate problem. We think of father in contrast to mother and fear that the creed is patriarchal in intent. For the first Christians who framed the creed, that was not the contrast they had in mind. God as a personal father was being contrasted to God as an impersonal substance. Patriarchy was taken for granted in the context of that culture, but it was not what was being taught. Parenthood was what the text of the creed asserted.

For the compilers of the Apostles' Creed, God was Father or parent in two senses. The first and most important, in the setting of the early church, was the affirmation that God was the Father of Jesus Christ. The creed has a Trinitarian pattern, and the central focus is on Jesus. The creed begins with the Jewish and Christian monotheistic assertion that God is one. The very next thing of necessity to say is that Jesus Christ is of the same essence with God. The biblical language used to assert this says that God is Father—the father of Jesus Christ. Jesus is not a creature, different from God. Neither is Jesus an adopted son, chosen and loved but of different parentage. It was essential for the early Christians in both the Nicene and the Apostles' creeds to assert that Jesus had an intimate, organic, essential relationship with God. Their way of saying it was that God was the father of Jesus Christ.

God is also *our* father. The setting in which the creed initially was learned and recited was Baptism. The new Christian believer vicariously experienced death as sin and rebirth as new life. The imagery is that of a child being born and thus bonded to a parent. Augustine, in a sermon on the creed, exclaimed, "Observe how quickly the words are spoken, and how full of significance they are. He is God, and He is Father: God in power, Father in goodness. How blessed we are who find that our Lord God is our Father."

Almighty. This father is also Almighty. Here again we are in danger of misunderstanding the intent of the early authors and users of the creed. For twentieth-century Americans, "almighty" immediately raises the specter of unlimited and possibly arbitrary use of infinite physical might. Nuclear weapons seem almighty. Early Christians were not thinking at all in those terms. The Greek word *pantokratōr* is not well rendered by the Latin *omnipotens* or by our modern sense of "almighty." The original meaning of the creed was "all-ruling," "all-sovereign." God was being acknowledged as the creator of all things and the ruler over all people.

Pagan philosophers such as Celsus (second century A.D.) seized on misinterpreted scraps of Christian doctrine and gave the impression that Christians taught that their God could do anything. Then it was possible to play the philosophical game of asking if God could create a weight heavier than God could lift. Augustine, in reply, turned Christian attention away from riddles based on cause and effect to the constancy of God's character. Augustine pointed to God's having the practical power to forgive all people's sins. Then he elaborated by saying, "I can tell the sort of things He cannot do. He cannot die, He cannot sin, He cannot lie, He cannot be deceived. Such things He cannot: if He could, He would not be almighty."

Creator—Maker of Heaven and Earth

Consistent with the assertions that God is one and that God is the Father of all living, God is also proclaimed to be the creator of all things. The phrase "Maker of heaven and earth" is not found in the early form of the creed, the Old Roman Symbol. For the first Christians, the notion of creator was bound up with the term "Father." Gradually, in response to heretical denials of Christ's essential sonship, the term "Father" in the creed took on the almost exclusive meaning of the Father of Jesus Christ. As the text of the creed was later elaborated in France in the fifth through seventh centuries, Christian teachers felt obliged to add the term "maker" to ensure the affirmation of God as the sole creator of all that existed.

The fact that God created heaven and earth and all things, visible and invisible, set Christianity apart from all other religions. The Latin translation of the Apostles' Creed uses the word "Creator" rather than "Maker." The reference to Genesis 1:1 is clear: "In the beginning God created the heavens and the earth."

Genesis is not interested in science in our sense of the term; it is concerned with something more basic. Genesis refutes polytheism. God is one. God created everything, including the heavens and the earth. The moon and the stars are not gods, as some Eastern religions claimed them to be. Nothing on the earth was to be worshipped as divine, not groves of trees, or birds, or sea monsters, or animals, or other men or women, as some of Israel's neighbors did. God alone is the creator. All the rest are creatures. God alone is to be worshipped and served. It is idolatry to give ultimate allegiance to any created thing.

"Maker of heaven and earth" rejects the deification of things. It also affirms the goodness of God's creation. At times, in early Christian history, this section of the creed was used to refute Gnosticism, with its denial that this material world was made by the good God. It also rejected Manichaeism, which made spirit good but matter evil. Christians at their theological best have never been anti-world or anti-body. Indeed, the creed climaxes with the conviction of "the resurrection of the body; and the life everlasting." This world, and we, are so good as God created us that we look forward to our very flesh being resurrected, and we begin to live now a new quality of life which will be everlasting.

Contemporary Relevance

Inclusive Language

Betty Friedan, speaking to a rally in New York City on Women's Liberation Day, August 26, 1970, declared, "I think that the great debate of the 1970s will be 'Is God He?'" Her nineteenth-century suffragist predecessor Emmeline Pankhurst had long before resolved that problem. She exhorted her followers, "Trust in God: *She* will provide!" Friedan's prediction came true a decade later for Presbyterians. With the publication, in 1983 and 1984, of Years A and B of the National Council of Churches' *Inclusive-Language Lectionary* (Year C will be out in 1985), an avalanche of words has been poured out regarding appropriate language about God and human beings. For some it is a conflict between radical feminist politics and traditional biblical texts. For others it is a confusion over the relationship between the Bible, various kinds of translations of the

Bible, lectionary readings from the Bible, and teaching about the Bible.

"Inclusive language" is a phrase, at its simplest, designed to indicate language that includes both women and men and uses female as well as male metaphors for God. A lectionary is a set of Bible passages prepared to be read aloud during public worship. There is usually one reading each from the Old Testament, the Epistles, and the Gospels for every Sunday of the year. The intent of a lectionary is to cover most of the Bible during a year, in an order appropriate to the seasons of the church year and including all the major themes of the Bible. Many Protestants, perhaps most, are unfamiliar with lectionaries. Presbyterians increasingly have turned to their use to prevent a one-sided dwelling on certain biblical themes to the exclusion of others.

The *Inclusive-Language Lectionary* published by the National Council of Churches has no authority in any of the member churches. It was offered as an experiment to see if such a rendition of biblical language would prove helpful in clarifying the intent of the Bible to speak to all people. The committee preparing the lectionary made changes in three areas.

First, language about people was changed. "Man" or "men" as generic terms were avoided when the intent of the text was to refer to "a person" or "people." Further, where roles for women could be inferred, their names were added in brackets and italicized. "We have Abraham as our Father [*and Sarah and Hagar as our mothers*]" is an example.

Second, language about Jesus Christ was changed. While recognizing that Jesus was, historically, a man, the lectionary editors sought to emphasize that Jesus' humanity, not his maleness, is decisive for the salvation of all people. For example, the lectionary uses "Child of God" rather than "Son of God."

Third, language about God was changed. The word

"God" is often used instead of the pronoun "he." Female imagery for God is inserted in brackets and italics, such as "God the Father [*and Mother*]." Traditionally patriarchal terms such as "Lord" and "King" are abandoned for more inclusive terms such as "Sovereign."

The language used in the confessional documents does not settle the issue of the appropriateness of inclusive language one way or the other. The crucial issue is how the confessions, or any other noncontemporary documents, are to be interpreted. We will say more, when dealing with the doctrine of Scripture in the confessions, about Reformed guidelines for interpreting Scripture. For now we need remember only this: What is at stake is not what the words are but our theory about the way words are to be used.

Our concern, initially, is not interpretation but translation. However, we soon discover that the two issues cannot be separated. All translation is, in a sense, interpretation. The purpose of translating texts is not just to preserve words but to clarify meaning. The words of Scripture were originally written in Hebrew, Aramaic, and Greek. The words of the Reformed confessions were originally written in Greek, Latin, German, and often archaic English. When these texts are translated from the original language to contemporary English, a change has occurred; we no longer have the original words. Someone has made a decision as to what word or words will best express the meaning of the source language of the original author in the receptor language of the contemporary reader or hearer.

Even the same language changes significantly over time. For example, in seventeenth-century English Jesus says, "Suffer little children to come unto me." "Suffer" simply meant "let" them come; we no longer use the word in that sense. Similarly, Paul, in King James English, speaks of a "let" to his ministry. Today, we only use "let" in the sense of "hindrance" in the game of tennis, when we speak of a "let" ball, one that hit the net as it went over. Our choice, in dealing with noncontemporary documents in outmoded or other languages from our own is never whether to keep the original words or not but which contemporary words best express the meaning of the original authors.

The debate over inclusive language does not rage only between feminists and fundamentalists. There is also a vigorous debate among reputable scholars over competing theories of translation. It can be a debate between philologists and linguists. Philology, in which most of us were trained, takes its models from the Western classical languages of Greek and Latin. The primary concern of philologists is a scholarly one—to find the single best word in contemporary English to represent the original word in the source language. Faithfulness to the original text is their stated objective. They focus on words.

Linguists take their models from non-Western languages. Most American-trained linguists have, for example, studied Native American languages such as Navajo, which are structurally different from Western languages. Their primary concern is that of the communicator—to find whatever words and phrases are necessary in contemporary English to convey the meaning of the original language in something of its dynamic force. The need of the contemporary reader or hearer to understand and respond to the message is their basic concern. They emphasize meaning.

The Revised Standard Version and the King James Version of the Bible are examples of translations based on philology. The *Good News Bible: The Bible in Today's English Version,* published by the American Bible Society, is a translation based on linguistics. Understandably, the *Good News Bible* more often uses inclusive language because it is oriented to contemporary English usage. Interestingly, linguistics is the base from which most translation of Scripture into non-Western languages is now being done. The Bible societies and groups such as Wycliffe Bible Translators have succeeded in bringing some part of the Bible to over 1,700 of the world's 6,000 languages.

Presbyterians, typically, have shown both scholarly openness and ecclesiastical reserve in dealing with questions of inclusive language. Two major studies of language about people and about God were made beginning in 1973. The two reports are available in a resource document entitled *The Power of Language Among the People of God and the Language About God, "Opening the Door."* The General Assembly in 1984 took two actions reflective of this dual attitude of openness and caution. It received for further study and experimentation (rather than adopted) the National Council of Churches' *Inclusive-Language Lectionary.* And in a report on baptism it recommended that the denomination continue to baptize "in the name of the Father and of the Son and of the Holy Spirit." The General Assembly did not find either of two alternative inclusive-language formulas acceptable yet as substitutes—"Creator-Redeemer-Sustainer," or "Shepherd-Helper-Refuge." Father, Son, and Spirit are references to who God is, while the other designations refer to what God does, and thus they are not interchangeable.

"I am God and not man, the Holy One in your midst" (Hos. 11:9). God is not a man. Nor is God a woman. God is the Holy One about whom we can speak only in symbols, analogies, and metaphors. Presbyterians will need to do much more study and experimentation to settle the issue of the appropriate inclusiveness of language about God. The confessions do not preclude that study but rather, encourage it by their example of putting biblical images and concepts into the contemporary language of the people and into new thought forms which have dynamic, life-changing power.

Creationism

In the last two decades, some fundamentalist groups have revived the controversy of the 1920s over creation and evolution. In the 1960s, efforts were made at first through legislative channels to prohibit the teaching of evolution in the science curricula of the public schools. A 1968 U.S. Supreme Court decision ruled such statutes unconstitutional as a violation of the First Amendment. Next, the move was made to require that what was called "the Genesis account of creation" receive equal time in classroom discussions and equal space in science textbooks. By early 1980, at least thirty-three such bills had been introduced in the legislatures of some eleven states. The assumption of those sponsoring such bills was that Genesis gave a scientific account of *how* the earth was created, including the notions that the earth is relatively young (10,000 to 12,000 years old) and that a series of catastrophes, such as great floods, could explain the earth's geology.

When matters of biblical interpretation are tried in the civil courts they take on many added complexities: legal, political, social, and psychological. If the political decisions of legislatures or the legal decisions of courts determine what the right interpretation of the Bible is to be, what is to hinder the dictation of our religion by whatever sect has the most money, the most sophisticated lobby, or the greatest ability to pressure those who make the laws?

One can certainly sympathize with persons on both sides of the creationist-evolutionist controversy. It is wrong for persons, in the name of science, dogmatically to rule out God as the ultimate creator of all that exists. Such persons are engaged in religious speech, dealing with matters of faith that go beyond the capability of scientific description. At the same time, one must be concerned that scientists have the freedom to use the best methods available in doing their research and to draw the conclusions that seem to them most warranted. Science, at its best, attempts to understand and explain the rules that govern the physical world in which we live and should not be hindered in its legitimate tasks.

The Reformed confessions give no support to the notion

that Genesis offers a scientific description of how the world was made. Theologians from the period of the early church down through the era of the Protestant Reformation believed that the overriding purpose of Scripture was to provide guidance on how to become rightly related to God and to our fellow human beings. The Reformed confessions uniformly say that Scripture speaks about salvation, faith, and life. Science is never mentioned.

It hardly could be, for what we know as modern science did not begin until almost the seventeenth century. Only our two twentieth-century confessions were written after this development. Isaac Newton was born in 1642, the year that Galileo died and the year before the Westminster Assembly of Divines (which wrote the Westminster Confession of Faith) was assembled. Science was not really widely practiced in England until after 1662, with the incorporation of the Royal Society of London for Improving Natural Knowledge. The word "scientist" was only introduced into the English language around 1840. In its present highly specialized form, science is virtually a twentieth-century phenomenon. *The International Encyclopedia of the Social Sciences* declares that "the scientists living in 1960 probably constituted more than 90 per cent of all those who ever lived." Those "scientists" who lived prior to the twentieth century were few and would be considered amateurs, compared to the highly trained professionals of today. Scientists, for us, are persons of great prestige whose activities provide standard means of explaining the world we live in and enabling us to live in it more comfortably. It is no wonder, therefore, that some people impose our present cultural commitment to science on everything we encounter, including the Bible. That was not the mentality of the biblical writers or of the authors of the Reformed confessions.

If we allow the Apostles' Creed to serve as a summary of the main themes of Scripture, we will avoid the problems raised by creationism. The rule of faith, which the creed elaborates, speaks of the following: God's good creation, humankind's fall into sin, God's merciful redemption in Jesus Christ, God's continuing rule through the Holy Spirit in the church, and the final hope of resurrection. The church has understood the function of the first eleven chapters of Genesis to be that of a theological prologue to this drama of redemption which is the theme of Scripture as a whole. The first three chapters of Genesis express this theme of creation, fall, and redemption in relation to the creation of the world and humankind. Genesis 1 is a Hebrew poem which uses a characteristic Near Eastern parallel structure. The light of the first day of creation is paired with the light givers (sun, moon, and stars) of the fourth day. The sky and seas of day two are paired with the birds and fish of day five. The land and vegetation of day three are paired with the animals and humanity of day six. And on the seventh day, God rested, because it was perfect.

God created. Nothing in creation is worthy of divine honor or our ultimate commitment. All of God's creation is good. These are the theological affirmations of Genesis 1. That is how the writers of the ecumenical creeds and the Reformed confessions looked at it. We would do well to learn from the Apostles' Creed that the central affirmations of Scripture relate to salvation and the Christian life. A right relation to God and to our neighbor will give us perspective on all of life, including science. And it will prevent us from imposing our cultural priorities on the more essential biblical verities.

II

Reformation Confessions

5

The Scots Confession
A.D. 1560

The Scots Confession is the first Reformed confession in the English language. It has been called the charter of the Church of Scotland and of world Presbyterianism.

This confession assumes, and was adapted to the needs of, a world we have never experienced. Medieval Roman Catholicism was the only recognized religion in sixteenth-century Scotland. Separation of church and state, in our modern sense, was unknown. The Protestant Reformation was a dynamic force changing the character of national politics as well as churchly piety on the European continent.

It was the Scottish Parliament, at the conclusion of a civil war, which invited John Knox and five colleagues to prepare a confession of faith for the church and the nation. They did their work in four days. The style of the document bears the marks of haste, but the content was not hastily conceived. The Scots Reformers had been preparing themselves and their thoughts for a long time. The First Helvetic Confession (1536) had been brought from Switzerland to Scotland by George Wishart and published there in English in 1548. John Knox had studied with John Calvin in Geneva and with other Reformed theologians in Switzerland.

The Scots wished to show their continuity with Christians of the ancient church. The structure of the Scots Confession parallels that of the Apostles' Creed. The twenty-five chapters of the confession are developed in sequence around the themes of Father, Son, Spirit, Church, and Consummation. The Scots also recognized and responded positively to the doctrinal standards of the Reformed churches of the Continent. Knox and his friends did not think that what they were doing was unique. Rather, they were applying already known Christian principles, with a Reformed perspective, to their particular national setting.

The Scots Confession of 1560 remained the doctrinal standard of the Church of Scotland until 1647. At that time it was superseded by the Westminster Confession of Faith, drawn up in England with the help of Scots commissioners. Again, the aim was continuity with the Reformed community: in this case, uniformity of confession, worship, and government for all churches in Great Britain. (It was the Westminster Confession which was brought to America in the seventeenth century.) We will discover a greater continuity with our Reformed and Scottish forebears as we come to know this first confession of Anglo-Saxon Presbyterianism.

Historical Context: The Case of the Scots Confession

It was August 17, 1560. John Knox felt that if the Scottish Parliament did not act soon, the chance to establish a Reformed confession of faith as the creed of Scotland might be lost forever. Years of bitter fighting and much bloodshed lay behind them, but the crucial test was still ahead.

In the previous four days, Knox and five friends had written a confession designed to solidify Scotland politically and ecclesiastically. They hoped that the nation would henceforth fly a Protestant flag, emblazoned with the cross of Saint Andrew. Now they waited. Would Parliament adopt their Protestant statement as the Scots Confession of Faith? Would the military victory just won over France open the way for the firm establishment of a Reformed Protestant church and nation?

Intrigue and Infamy: The Sixteenth-Century Context

Mid-sixteenth-century Europe was a highly unstable place of rampant suspicion and rapidly shifting centers of power. Philip II of Spain held the reins of the most powerful centralized government in Western Europe. In France, a series of weak monarchs had been succeeded by a regency commanded by Catherine de' Medici, who found herself caught in a tug-of-war between the politically powerful Guise family and the Bourbon family. In England, Elizabeth I reigned. The daughter of Henry VIII and Anne Boleyn, she was by birth and preference a Protestant. The English remembered only too well the fiery deaths of Protestant martyrs Nicholas Ridley, Hugh Latimer, and Thomas Cranmer during the reign of their recent Roman Catholic monarch, the infamous Mary Tudor.

Elizabeth's cousin Mary Stuart was crowned Queen of Scotland when she was just six days old. Mary was the only daughter of James V of Scotland, who died days after his daughter's birth, leaving the government in the hands of his French second wife, the Roman Catholic Mary of Guise. So the infant had links to the thrones of both France and England (where she had the strongest claim after the children of Henry VIII) and was thus both a threat and a rival to the unmarried Elizabeth. A chief diplomatic goal of the French king was to capture the English throne, in pursuit of which he sought a marriage to secure young Mary's claim. English Catholics supported these efforts, treating Elizabeth as an illegitimate ruler because the pope had never recognized Henry VIII's divorce from Catherine of Aragon or sanctified his marriage to Anne Boleyn.

Political alliances between France, Spain, England, and Scotland were tenuous at best. England courted Spanish favor to prevent dangerous Catholic liaisons. France mistrusted both England and powerful Spain, a feeling that was returned. Protestant Scots allied themselves with Elizabeth's court, while English Catholics upheld Mary Stuart's royal aspirations.

Two related fears dominated the political scene in Scotland during this period. One was fear of annexation by Protestant England, which would sever Scottish ties with Catholic France. The other was fear of French infiltration into the Scottish court and the consequent bleeding of Scotland's already scant resources. Mary Stuart was the pawn in these political intrigues but was not personally present. In August of 1548, less than six years old, she was sent to France, not to return for thirteen years. Her mother, Mary of Guise, ruled Scotland as regent.

The Light of Burning Martyrs: Hamilton and Wishart

The Roman Catholic Church in Scotland had long been corrupt. Ecclesiastical posts were doled out to the idle sons of wealthy nobles in exchange for money and power. The clergy were largely illiterate and did not bother to preach. Need for reform was obvious. To quench dissatisfaction among the people, the church began to appoint laymen as bishops and abbots. At this time, Lutheran writings were being smuggled into Scottish seaport towns such as Dundee. Here and there, lay preachers began to question the church's authority.

Persuaded by Lutheran doctrine, one of these men, Patrick Hamilton, began to preach reformation. On February 28, 1528, Hamilton was summoned to St. Andrews, the religious capital of Scotland, and "invited" to debate his views with the notorious archbishop, Cardinal David Beaton. In reality, Beaton had convened a kangaroo court of his most influential friends: Hamilton was charged with heresy, convicted, and publicly burned at dawn the next day. Beaton had intended to quell the rising tide of the Scottish Reformation, but many people questioned the obvious haste of Hamilton's trial, and an anti-Catholic reaction ensued. As one bystander observed, "The reek of smoke from Mr. Hamilton's body has infected as many as it did blow upon." One of those "infected" that day at St. Andrews was a young teacher named George Wishart.

Wishart prepared himself for effective action. He traveled to Geneva, where he studied with Calvin. In 1543, he returned to Scotland and began preaching Reformed doctrine. So stirred were some of the people who heard Wishart that they rushed out to destroy the nearest monasteries.

This was not unrest, it was revolt. Cardinal Beaton was determined once and for all to end this "reform heresy"; his men pursued Wishart, who eluded the corrupt cardinal by fleeing from town to town, yet preaching at every stop. In the village of Haddington, Wishart met a young tutor named John Knox. Knox was profoundly influenced and asked to accompany Wishart. But the preacher sensed impending danger. He charged Knox to return to his pupils, saying, "One is sufficient for a sacrifice." Wishart's intuition was correct. Just five hours later, he was captured by an army of five hundred of Beaton's men.

Wishart was charged with eighteen counts of heresy by Beaton's hand-picked tribunal, and on February 29, 1546, with every cannon of St. Andrews Castle loaded and aimed at him, he was burned to death. Cardinal Beaton watched the proceedings from the castle wall, his plump body reclining on cushions. What he did not yet know was that he had not simply burned a heretic. He had lit the fire of rebellion.

One cool morning in May 1546, a little band of desperate Protestants, under the leadership of a man named John Lesslie, broke into the castle, quickly seized control, and ran their swords through Cardinal Beaton. Wishart's and Hamilton's deaths had been avenged. Now they needed someone to preach the gospel for which these martyrs had died. They chose John Knox.

John Knox: The Preacher of God's Good News

John Knox was born around 1514 at Haddington, a small town on the chilly east coast of Scotland. At age seventeen he began to study theology at St. Andrews University. He was ordained a Catholic priest in 1536.

The next seven years were quiet ones, routinely spent, first in priestly duties and then as tutor to two boys. Around 1542, Knox first heard the reformed preaching of Thomas Gwilliam. Then, in 1544, he met George Wishart. Knox adopted Wishart's vision of the prophetic vocation as well as his Calvinistic stance.

After Wishart's death, Knox joined the band of Protestant rebels at St. Andrews as their chaplain. His ministry was cut short, however, by the arrival of French warships blockading the harbor and castle. The castle fell. Knox was seized and held as a galley slave in the French fleet. For nineteen months he was chained to an oar, half naked and often near death. Intervention by the English government brought his release in 1549. Returned to England, Knox began preaching in earnest.

Knox took a post as pastor in Berwick, an English town near the Scottish border with a reputation for violence and immorality. Here, he hit his stride, preaching against the Mass and the "harlot" Roman Church and establishing himself as a person to be reckoned with. Several times Knox was asked to defend his views before magistrates in Northumberland and London. Although the Privy Council of London contained a number of Protestant sympathizers, Knox was told that they were sorry his mind lay contrary to the common order. "I am more sorry," he replied, "that the common order is contrary to the institution of Jesus Christ."

It soon became clear that, if he stayed in England, Knox would have to choose between acceptance of the Mass and a martyr's fate. In January of 1554, he fled to Geneva. There he met with Calvin, who was not enthusiastic about some of the Scotsman's revolutionary ideas. Knox, however, was most impressed by what he saw of Calvin's model regime. "It is the most perfect school of Christ that ever was on earth since the days of the apostles," he wrote.

Despite his absence from Berwick, Knox did not cease exhorting his followers to stand firm against the Catholic Church. As soon as he felt safe, Knox slipped back into Scotland and began to whip the Protestant coalition into fighting form. Mary of Guise, the queen-mother regent, ordered him tried for heresy. Six days before the trial was scheduled to begin, she mysteriously dropped the charges. Knox seized this opportunity to preach openly and boldly in Edinburgh. At the same time he wrote to Mary encouraging her to turn Protestant. Mary ridiculed Knox's attempt to convert her by burning him in effigy in Edinburgh. Knox was unmoved. It was 1555. The Protestant movement was gaining momentum.

By 1557, Knox was once again in serious danger, so he returned to Geneva, where he spent a year studying and writing. Two of his most famous works came from this period: *Predestination* and *The First Blast of the Trumpet Against the Monstrous Regiment of Women.* The latter, a diatribe against all women rulers, enraged Elizabeth I, and she refused him safe passage through England. Knox clearly knew his need for English support. He later modified his view of "monstrous" women monarchs and extolled Elizabeth as a "Deborah," a peerless prophetess. Elizabeth's anger was mollified, and she smiled on Knox and supported his Reformed movement once again.

On May 2, 1559, Knox finally returned to Scotland. That day, the Catholic clergy of Edinburgh had assembled to discuss implementing certain reforms in an attempt to pacify their parishioners. Specifically, if any priest were found in open adultery, he would lose a third of his income property at the first offense. (The fact that Cardinal Beaton had had eight illegitimate children went unmentioned.)

Just ten days after Knox's return, Mary of Guise decreed

that every Protestant preacher must stand before her at Stirling. Knox replied that Mary would have to receive all his congregation—with every man armed—or he would not come. The regent asked her daughter, Mary Stuart, now married to French royalty, to dispatch French troops. Knox preached his way from Edinburgh to Stirling, in direct defiance of the archbishop's threat to shoot him on sight. Along the way, fourteen priests were converted to Protestantism.

The time was ripe for revolution. Supporting troops arrived from England. Together with the Scottish rebels, they laid siege to the French stronghold at Leith. On June 11, 1560, Mary of Guise died, and with her went the exiled Mary Stuart's cause. On July 6, a treaty was signed between France and England stipulating France's complete withdrawal from Scotland and noninterference with its government.

The revolution had succeeded, but with the help of England; Scotland still had not achieved national independence. Knox urged the Scottish Parliament to adopt a confession of faith that would unify the country politically and ecclesiastically.

The Scots Confession: August 17, 1560

> Long have we thirsted, dear brethren, to make known to the world the sum of that doctrine which we profess and for which we have sustained infamy and danger. But such has been the rage of Satan against us, and against Jesus Christ's eternal verity, lately now born again among us, that to this day no time has been granted us to clear our consciences, as most gladly we would have done. For how we have been tossed until now the most part of Europe, we suppose, understands.

With these impassioned words, Knox introduced his Scots Confession, hoping to demonstrate its solidarity with the confessions of the Reformed churches of the Continent. He sought Parliament also to give formal recognition to the doctrinal standards of Geneva and Zurich.

For Knox, the chief obstruction to reformation was the position taken by the Roman Catholic Church at Trent in 1546. The Counter-Reformation Council of Trent maintained that justification consisted not only of remission of sins but of the sanctification and renovation of the inner being by supernatural love. For this, faith alone was not enough. People had to cooperate with the church by participating in its sacraments. Observation of the Mass was central to the Catholic view of justification. The Mass was the center of the mystery of salvation, a commemoration but also a real and present sacrifice of Christ on the cross.

Election. In the Scots Confession, Knox specifically denied the sacrificial character of the Mass. For him, abolition of the Mass was essential if people were truly to trust in Christ and his grace alone by faith for their salvation. Knox's answer was election. God alone was able to save his people. In his great mercy, he elected—chose—them to salvation; they did not achieve it by human means. Human sin was no match for the mercy of God's grace.

For Knox, election was not something arbitrary but was intimately tied to Jesus Christ, who was our brother, chosen by God to suffer for our sakes. In Chapter VIII, the Scots Confession declared:

> That same eternal God and Father, who by grace alone chose us in his Son Christ Jesus before the foundation of the world was laid, appointed him to be our head, our brother, our pastor, and the great bishop of our souls. . . . Further, it behooved the Messiah and Redeemer to be true God and true man, because he was able to undergo the punishment of our transgressions and to present himself in the presence of his Father's judgment, as in our stead, to suffer for our transgression and disobedience, and by death to overcome him that was the author of death.

The Church. The elect are gathered into the church. Chapters II through V of the Scots Confession outlined the history of the church from Adam to Christ, a history of human salvation. Chapter XVIII designated the three marks of the True Kirk: the true preaching of the Word, the right administration of the Sacraments, and upright administration of ecclesiastical discipline. Election and church were tied together in the Scots Confession by the notion that not all in the visible church necessarily belong to the true church. God's grace and not human action was finally the basis for salvation and incorporation into God's community.

The Scots Confession closed on a militant and triumphant note:

> Arise, O Lord, and let thine enemies be confounded; let them flee from thy presence that hate thy godly Name. Give thy servants strength to speak thy Word with boldness, and let all nations cleave to the true knowledge of thee. Amen.

Lifting his eyes from these words, John Knox—the man who was said to fear no one but God—turned and looked at the five men who had helped him write this confession during the past four days. Knox knew well the sacrifice and suffering which had brought them to this moment. He believed that the welfare of both the nation and the church hung in the balance. Then he heard the presiding officer of Parliament call for a vote on the adoption of the Scots Confession.

Essential Tenets of the Reformed Faith

Election

Election is the Reformed way of saying grace alone. Knox and his Reformed predecessors were saying the same thing that Luther was proclaiming in his central affirmation of justification by grace through faith. Both were following the great theologian of the early church, Augustine, who stressed human sinfulness and the inability of people to change their hearts unless God first acted to change them. Chapter VIII of the Scots Confession uses the phrase "grace alone," and Chapter XII speaks of salvation "without respect to any merit proceeding from us."

Dutch Reformed theologian Gerrit C. Berkouwer has written about the "comfort of election." Election is a doctrine of assurance for us. It tells us that what God has done in mercy we cannot undo, even by our worst sins. It is not a doctrine to use in evangelism. It is a doctrine designed to provide comfort and induce humility in believers. It is a doctrine for Christians at the end of their lives who look back and give glory to God for what God has done, knowing that they were not in sole control.

Someone has said jokingly that all people should be Methodists before they are converted and Presbyterians afterward. Before conversion, all we need to know is that if we are willing to trust God in Christ, we can be saved. The Methodist stress on free will is appropriate here. But after we are converted, we should fall on our knees and say, "Thank you, God, that you were merciful to me, a sinner!" A Presbyterian stress on God's gracious action before we acted is appropriate here. Presbyterians believe that, from God's perspective, both these appropriate affirmations fit together harmoniously. When we try to rationalize their relationship, however, we usually end up distorting one reality or the other. It is better that we be faithful to what Scripture teaches, and apply it to the context where it fits, than to try to force it into a neat, humanly logical package.

The Church

The church is both invisible and visible. It is meaningful to speak of the church, as the Scots Confession does, and mean the universal church, including all those whom God has graciously touched in all times and all places. This church began with Adam, says Chapter V of the confession. It includes those who yet live and those who will live hereafter. This is the invisible church, "known only to God," as Chapter XVI indicates. But there are visible expressions of that invisible church. It is with what the Scots Confession calls "particular Kirks" that we primarily have to do. They include churches in places such as "Corinth, Galatia, Ephesus, and . . . the realm of Scotland," as Chapter XVIII of the confession notes. They include the First and Second and last Presbyterian Church on any street in the United States. It is to these visible churches that the marks of the "True Kirk" are to be applied.

For most of Protestantism, and for most of the Reformed community, even for Calvin, there are two marks of the true church. If the Word of God is truly preached and the sacraments of Communion and Baptism are rightly administered, there is a true church. John Knox added a third criterion, understandable considering the corruption in the church against which he was protesting. Knox said that a third mark of the church was "ecclesiastical discipline uprightly ministered."

We have all heard stories of excesses of church discipline in Presbyterianism's past. We frown on attempts to "fence the table," forbidding any but those judged righteous by the session to come to Communion. We are horrified at the human error (and often spite) involved in the public disciplining of church members, which we associate with the Puritanism of early America.

Presbyterians still have an elaborate system of discipline. If we are to be responsible, we must use it. In the Presbyterian system we do not turn our judgment over to some individual. Elected representatives of congregations, presbyteries, synods, and General Assembly from time to time have to take the heavy responsibility of exercising disciplinary judgment, both in matters of doctrine and of morals.

Without that we would have no system of Presbyterian government, only an anarchy of arbitrary activity. Our system of discipline is designed to protect the rights of each individual and to ensure the orderly working of the community. It is meant to enable minority voices to be heard and still to allow the will of the majority to function. Ecclesiastical discipline is still part of what it means to be Presbyterian.

Contemporary Relevance

Election in an Era of Freedom

Election or, as it is sometimes called, predestination, seems to be a hard doctrine for many contemporary Presbyterians. Part of that is because in our day we place a premium on individual freedom. We know that we are subject to the predetermination of our genes and the formative influences of our early environment, yet still we believe that we are free. And so we should. As human beings we are the products of our heredity and our environment, and yet we are not reducible to those factors alone. We are independent, morally responsible persons. We are free.

Reformed theology means to say the same thing about God's fore-choice and our free moral responsibility. It is not a case of either/or but of both/and. The doctrine of election gives us a good exercise in learning to do theology in specific situations and out of pastoral concern, and not merely in a mechanical manner. The pastoral questions are: How does this apply to us? What do we need to know? Then the answers make sense. If we trust and believe, God will always receive us. That is a genuinely biblical promise. And when we know ourselves to be so received, then we realize it was because of God's grace, not because of our own virtue or action. That is equally true.

Physicists speak of light as waves or as particles (tiny

pieces of matter or energy). They know that light is not two things but one reality. It is just that under certain experimental conditions light appears as waves, and under other experimental conditions light seems to be composed of particles. So in theology we must realize that though we are handling holy things, our descriptions rely on very human analogies. As the prophet Isaiah declares, we are not capable of knowing as God knows (Isa. 55:8). But God has given us in Scripture what we need to know in a very human form that we can understand. Reformed theologians have spoken of God's adaptation, condescension, accommodation to our human capacity so that we might understand how to relate to God and to one another. That is what the incarnation is all about—God coming to us in human form. Our theological reflection on the biblical stories of a very real God's interaction with real people must take into account the context, the characters, and the manner in which there is an application to us. We must find where we fit rather than wanting to know the future from God's perspective.

Discipline in a Day of Self-indulgence

Discipline is a disagreeable word to some. It is not to athletes preparing for the Olympics. For them, discipline is the key to releasing their full potential. Discipline was not a dirty word to the writers of the Scots Confession. They saw life as a continual struggle against very difficult odds. They needed strength, preparedness, alertness, all the abilities that discipline gives in order to meet the challenges of living the Christian life. In their view, life became more difficult, not easier, when one became a Christian. Listen to their description of the life of faith:

> Thence comes that continual battle which is between the flesh and the Spirit in God's children. . . . Other men do not share this conflict since they do not have God's Spirit, but they readily follow and obey sin and feel no regrets,

> since they act as the devil and their corrupt nature urge. But the sons of God fight against sin; sob and mourn when they find themselves tempted to do evil; and if they fall, rise again with earnest and unfeigned repentance. They do these things, not by their own power, but by the power of the Lord Jesus, apart from whom they can do nothing. (Chapter XIII)

The picture of the Christian life given by popular Christian pietism tends to be just the opposite of the Scots Confession. Newspaper advertisements and mass-market paperback books offer a Christianity that will make life pleasant, prosperous, and pure. While we may not view the Christian way as quite so rocky as our Scottish forerunners, Presbyterians tend to take a realistic view of life as a mixture of good and evil, and of human nature as subject to sin. Therefore, we still need discipline.

The Book of Order of the Presbyterian Church (U.S.A.) provides for two kinds of cases subject to judicial action. There are remedial cases in which a person or a group alleges irregularity in the actions of a governing body, such as session or presbytery. There are also disciplinary cases in which a person or a governing body brings charges against an individual subject to the jurisdiction of the church: a minister, elder, deacon, or church member.

Perhaps the most widely discussed disciplinary cases are those involving the alleged sexual improprieties of a minister. They make the mot sensational newspaper copy, despite the fact that great care is taken to keep the proceedings secret to protect the rights and reputations of all persons involved. Presbyterians have highly diverse reactions to such cases. Some feel that such actions in the church courts are no longer appropriate. We should be mature, able to recognize human frailty and forgive. Others feel that standards have become far too lax, that there are no visible differences between the church and the world, and that much greater caution must be exercised.

Presbyterian law still takes the view of the Scots Confession that life is a struggle and that discipline is necessary and helpful for the individual and the community. In *The Problem Clergymen Don't Talk About,* Charles L. Rassieur, a pastoral counselor, recounted case histories and analyzed the problems of male clergy who were tempted to, or had, become sexually involved with parishioners. (The problem is certainly no less real for female clergy, but to date no significant studies have been done.) Rassieur exhibits real empathy with the built-in problems of the pastor's task as counselor. He acknowledges the vulnerability of those who necessarily become intimately involved in the personal lives of others. But the bottom line becomes responsibility. Rassieur states:

> Another essential point for coping effectively is for the pastor to take full responsibility for his emotional responses to counselees. Theological clarity requires the pastor to assume that kind of responsibility for himself. No set of circumstances precludes the basic nature of man as a choice maker. We are free to respond; and so radical is that freedom that we are even responsible, as Christians, for those dimensions of ourselves over which we seem to have little or no control. The views, "She seduced me," or, "She's so sexually aggressive I was helpless," are thinly veiled excuses for abdicating personal responsibility.

In 1982, the Council on Women and the Church of the former United Presbyterian Church in the U.S.A. produced a booklet, *Naming the Unnamed: Sexual Harassment in the Church.* It focused on the power dynamic involved when someone in a position of authority makes unwanted sexual advances or demands which are perceived by the recipient as demeaning, intimidating, or coercive. The booklet states, "Sexual harassment is a form of encounter which is dehumanizing for the victim. It involves an unwarranted misuse of power on the part of one person against the other."

In our present permissive culture, ministers and church members are continually told that they have a right to have their own needs met. The church, through its preaching and disciplinary process, reminds us that we have not only rights but responsibilities. When we accept those responsibilities, we become free and find help for the meeting of our own needs. The Scots Confession and Presbyterian practice are clear that when repentance follows sin there is forgiveness and restoration. The disciplinary process tests whether there is real repentance and whether the consequences of sin in the lives of others have been adequately confessed and compensated. Freedom is compatible with the doctrine of election. And discipline is integral to the Reformed doctrine of the church.

6

The Heidelberg Catechism
A.D. 1563

The Heidelberg Catechism was the first Reformed confession to appear in America. In 1609, less than a half century after its composition, Dutch explorers brought it to Manhattan Island. Thus, long before there was a New York City, the Dutch settlers of New Amsterdam were steeped in the Heidelberg Catechism, and when Presbyterians came to New York and the Middle Colonies, they found a Reformed presence that was congenial and receptive.

The adherents of the Scots Confession of 1560 knew and used the Heidelberg Catechism. It also became the chief theological standard for the Reformed communities in Hungary, Germany, and the Netherlands. Many of the courageous representatives of the Confessing Church in Germany, about whom we will learn in chapter 9, were nurtured on the Heidelberg Catechism, and it was approved by the General Assembly for use in Presbyterian congregations in the United States as early as 1870. In 1963, the Reformed Church in America sponsored a new English translation of the Heidelberg Catechism to celebrate the 400th anniversary of its publication. The 400th anniversary of the death of Zacharias Ursinus, one of the authors of the catechism, was marked in 1983.

Of all the Reformed confessions, the Heidelberg Catechism is the most personal. It is directed to the individual and to the individual's needs. The first question asks,

"What is your only comfort, in life and in death?" And the believer is enabled by the catechism to answer, "That I belong—body and soul, in life and in death—not to myself but to my faithful Savior, Jesus Christ." The question-and-answer style involves the person in reflecting and responding from the heart as well as the mind.

In Dutch Reformed congregations, typically, the catechism was taught to young people for several years during after-school sessions, preparing them for church membership. Pastors preached through the catechism each year, usually in the evening service, guided by the grouping of questions and answers in fifty-two Lord's Days. The Heidelberg Catechism offers a highly useful tool for instruction in the Christian faith, because it integrates into its text the Apostles' Creed, the Lord's Prayer, the Ten Commandments, and discussions of Baptism and Communion, all interpreted in a Reformed perspective.

Historical Context: The Case of the Heidelberg Catechism

Frederick III, elector of the Palatinate, stood in the center of the vast Council Hall of Augsburg, facing the Emperor Maximilian II. Around him stood six other electors and their advisers. The year was 1566. The emperor sat waiting to hear Elector Frederick's defense of the catechism he had adopted in 1563 in his Palatinate. Frederick was a good man, thought Maximilian, but stubborn. He had caused trouble by his introduction of a catechism not in agreement with the Augsburg Confession. His blatant encouragement of Calvinism—that had to stop, Maximilian mused. If Frederick refused, he might have to be banished from the empire . . . or worse.

Frederick's mind raced. Everything for which he had struggled in his seven years as governor of a small German province was now on the line. He asked himself two difficult questions. Could German Protestants maintain political unity in the face of bitter doctrinal disputes over the Lord's Supper? Would the truths put forth in the Heidelberg Catechism—truths in which Frederick deeply believed—be respected, or would they be banned by the Roman Catholics and the High Lutherans? Frederick was calm, but he knew he had to think quickly as he considered his response.

Controversy Over Communion

The Reformation in Germany became public in 1517 when Professor Martin Luther nailed ninety-five theses he was willing to debate to the door of the castle church in Wittenberg. Soon pockets of Protestant sympathy emerged in Heidelberg, Paris, Zürich, and elsewhere. But even as the new movement gained strength, divisions appeared. Controversy developed over key doctrinal issues. The most heated conflict centered on the sacrament of the Lord's Supper. Protestants split into three camps: Lutheran, Zwinglian, and Calvinist.

In 1529, Luther led German Protestants in debate against Swiss followers of Zwingli in the city of Marburg. Each side hoped to convince the other of the true nature of the sacraments. Luther's basic argument was rooted in a literal interpretation of a certain passage of Scripture. Jesus said, "This is my body," and that ended the matter for Luther. He was helped by a philosophical position which contended that since God was omnipotent, Christ's physical body could be present everywhere at once. For Luther, it was important to maintain that Christ's body was physically present in the bread and wine of the Lord's Supper.

Zwingli found Luther's position linguistically and philosophically in error. The word "is," in "This is my body," was for Zwingli clearly a figure of speech. Christ had been right there when he uttered those words at the last supper with his disciples. Furthermore, physical bodies can only be in one place at one time. According to the Bible, Zwingli argued, the resurrected body of Christ was in heaven. Therefore it could not be physically present in the Lord's Supper. The purpose of the supper was to remember Jesus as he had asked his disciples to do.

Both Lutherans and Zwinglians disagreed with another group of Reformed thinkers represented by Calvin. In a later development, the Calvinists argued that Christ was really present in the elements of Communion. That presence, however, was spiritual, not physical.

In Marburg, the debate proceeded in orderly fashion, but it soon became obvious that neither side had any intention of compromising. The Colloquy of Marburg was disbanded, leaving the question of the Lord's Supper unresolved. Each faction, upon returning home, became more obstinate than ever in its beliefs.

Frederick the Elector

High on a wooded hill overlooking the silvery Neckar River sat Heidelberg Castle, a medieval stone fortress encircled by a sixty-foot moat. Below it spread the town of Heidelberg, dominated by the spires of the Holy Ghost Church and the buildings of the ancient university, founded in 1386. Otto Henry was Protestant Elector of the Palatinate, a German province that encompassed Worms and had Heidelberg as its capital. In 1559, Otto Henry died childless. The crown of this prosperous and influential province then descended to his nephew, Frederick.

Frederick had been raised in the decadent Catholic court of Charles V, Holy Roman emperor. Disgusted by the bribery, drunkenness, and debauchery he saw around him, Frederick willingly converted to Protestantism in 1537, when he married Princess Maria of Brandenburg-Kulmbach, a devout High Lutheran. The High Lutherans were traditionalists who insisted on what they considered to be the original forms of Lutheran doctrine and liturgy. Maria made Frederick promise to read the Bible daily. He complied, spending many hours in study and reflection. As he did, he came to believe in salvation by grace, through faith. He began to pray directly to Jesus Christ. When Frederick went to Heidelberg as elector, at the age of forty-four, he was known as a pious and devout Protestant.

Uproar in Heidelberg

Once in Heidelberg, Frederick and Maria had scarcely unpacked their trunks before the new elector found himself embroiled in a bitter fracas between local Protestant factions. The chief instigator was the High Lutheran pastor of the Holy Ghost Church, arrogant, wild-tempered Tilemann Hesshus. The opposition to Hesshus rallied around Wilhelm Klebitz, a zealous Zwinglian who was assistant pastor.

The situation came to a head in the summer of 1559. Hesshus, in addition to being pastor of the church, was principal of the College of Wisdom, the theological training school. While Hesshus was absent, the faculty of the college awarded a theology degree to Klebitz (knowing that Hesshus would have forbidden this act had he been present). When he returned, Hesshus was furious. He preached a scathing sermon, calling Klebitz a Zwinglian devil and promising that this "hellish, devilish, cursed, cruel, and terrible thing" the learned faculty had done would be punished in frightening fashion unless the degree was revoked and Klebitz thrown out of the church and the Palatinate. To his great embarrassment, Hesshus was ignored. The following Sunday, Klebitz stood at the communion table, ready to assist as usual. But when he lifted the cup of wine, Hesshus wrenched it from his hand. The shocked congregation stared as its pastors skirmished in the chancel of the church.

Frederick sent both men packing, Klebitz with a recommendation, Hesshus without one. The issue of the sacraments was an explosive one, and Frederick wondered how he could bring peace to the Palatinate. He closed himself in his rooms to study the Bible. In Scripture, he hoped to see for himself God's answers to the questions that were tearing his province apart.

Lutheran Advice

Frederick had written to peace-loving Philip Melanchthon, Luther's trusted colleague and successor as leader of Lutheranism. In November of 1559, the answer from Melanchthon came: "In all things seek peace and moderation. This is done best by holding carefully to a fixed doctrinal position as regards the Lord's Supper and all other matters of faith." But *what* fixed doctrinal position? Frederick thought. He knew he must take a stand. The more he read, the more he leaned toward the Calvinists' view.

Princess Maria worried that her husband was moving too far from the "true" High Lutheran position. With the help of her son-in-law, she proposed a debate between two Lutherans and two scholars of Frederick's choice. Frederick agreed and chose Peter Boquin, a Calvinist, and Thomas Erastus, a Zwinglian. For two days the men discussed Holy Communion, and for another three days they debated the location and nature of the body of Christ. At the end, Frederick felt more strongly than ever that the Bible taught Calvin's version of the Reformed faith.

Six months later, in January 1561, Duke Christopher of Württemberg held a conference at Naumburg. He invited all the German dukes and princes to sign the Augsburg Confession as a declaration of their theological unity. The leaders were presented with two versions. The first was the original Augsburg Confession, written by Melanchthon to show that the Protestant faith was the faith of the ancient church. Its interpretation of the Lord's Supper was acceptable to the papal theologians when presented in 1530. The second version of the confession included *variata,* or changes, which Melanchthon introduced in 1540. The changes in Article X, on the Lord's Supper, had been warmly approved by Calvin himself. Frederick was able to persuade everyone present to sign the second version—everyone but his High Lutheran son-in-law.

Caspar Olevianus, the Preacher

Before Otto Henry's death in Heidelberg, Frederick and Maria had lived with their seven children in Trier, an ancient walled city on the Moselle River. Long a Catholic stronghold, the town's cathedral claimed to possess several priceless relics, including the holy coat of Christ and the bones of St. Matthew. In the same city was born Caspar Olevianus, son of a prosperous butcher. A bright lad, Olevianus was sent to study in France. There he befriended Herman Louis, eldest son of Frederick and Maria. One night the two were out with a party of drunken students who persuaded Herman Louis to cross the River Eure with them in a rickety rowboat. The boat overturned in midstream. Olevianus, watching from shore, swam out to save his friend, but he was too late. Frederick was devastated by his son's death but vowed never to forget the young man who had risked his life in a rescue attempt.

The river accident made Caspar Olevianus rethink his personal plans. Instead of being a lawyer, he would become a preacher. France was in the throes of Reformation. Olevianus was moved by the courage of persecuted French Protestants. He converted to Protestantism and traveled to Geneva to study with John Calvin. He also went to Lausanne, to meet Theodore Beza, and to Zürich, where he studied with Peter Martyr (Vermigli). When he returned to Geneva, he promised the fiery William Farel that he would take the Reformation faith back to Roman Catholic Trier.

In 1559, Olevianus returned home to Trier. He found a job teaching Latin in the local high school and chose the writings of Melanchthon as his textbook. The year 1559 was a pivotal year for Reformed Protestantism: French Protestants held their first synod meeting in Paris, John Knox returned to Scotland from Geneva, Calvin opened his Academy, and Elector Frederick began his rule in Heidelberg. Olevianus wanted to take a more active part, so he began to preach the Reformed faith publicly. His eloquence attracted huge crowds, and he was given St. Jacob's Church in which to preach. Day after day, the church was filled to overflowing. People sat on the altar and on the window ledges to hear. The town council was worried. What would happen if the archbishop found out? Olevianus was ordered to stop preaching. He refused.

Archbishop John found out, and he was furious. He arrived with his cavalry and laid siege to Trier. He burned the crops, barred the roads so farmers could not bring in produce, robbed any citizen who ventured outside the gates, and did his best to cut off the town water supply. On October 8, he ordered the Protestants to pay him 20,000 gold florins and leave Trier at once. When they refused, his troops stormed the city. They took possession of all Protestant property and threw Olevianus and twelve others into prison.

Olevianus had been in prison ten weeks when an emissary arrived from Frederick, in Heidelberg. This messenger from the new elector presented the archbishop with a trunkful of money and a written promise that Olevianus would not return to Trier if released; he presented Olevianus with an offer to preach in the Holy Ghost Church. The archbishop released the young preacher, who left immediately for Heidelberg.

Zacharias Ursinus, the Professor

Gentle, shy, and brilliant, young Zacharias Ursinus of Breslau had been discovered by Melanchthon. By his early twenties, Ursinus's academic prowess and serious manner had secured for him the headship of Breslau's Elizabethan School. Melanchthon had not been without influence, and by now some of his views had earned him the epithet of "crypto-Calvinist." Soon Ursinus was accused of being a Calvinist heretic instead of a true Lutheran.

Ursinus was a peaceful person and hated public argument. The growing conflict over the Lord's Supper and other issues made him increasingly uncomfortable. In 1560, Melanchthon died. Ursinus immediately resigned his post and went to Zürich to study with Peter Martyr (Vermigli), saying, "I am well content to leave my country when it will not tolerate the confession of truth which I cannot in good conscience give up."

Peter Martyr recognized in Ursinus a possible successor. Therefore, when Frederick wrote to the sixty-year-old scholar urging him to come to Heidelberg as principal of the College of Wisdom, Martyr made a counter offer. "I am too old to face a new challenge," he replied, "but we have here in Zürich the man you seek. His name is Zacharias Ursinus. He is only twenty-seven years old, but already he has the brilliance of a great scholar and the piety of a great servant of God. Send for him instead of me." And that is what Frederick did.

The New Catechism

Frederick knew that the time had come for a definitive statement of faith, one that would unify Reformed Protestants in the Palatinate and beyond. He gazed out the castle window at the town below. He had installed the eloquent and magnetic Olevianus of Trier as pastor of the Holy Ghost Church and had placed the brilliant scholar Ursinus in the College of Wisdom. Together they might be the ones to write a new catechism which would unite the Palatinate, instruct young Protestants, and apply biblical teaching to personal life. Frederick set the two men to work.

The resulting catechism was written in three main sections. The first dealt with sin and guilt. The second and longest part discussed redemption and freedom. The final section treated thankfulness to God in obedience and prayer.

Within this three-part framework, Olevianus and Ursinus incorporated questions and answers on the Apostles' Creed, Baptism, the Lord's Supper, the Ten Commandments, and the Lord's Prayer. The most controversial sections for High Lutherans and Roman Catholics were those on the Lord's Supper, which established clearly that the "sacred bread" did not become the "body of Christ."

In January of 1563, Frederick called the ministers and teachers of the Palatinate together to review the new catechism. After eight days of prayer and discussion, they unanimously approved it. Frederick charged everyone to remain faithful to its truths. Then he picked up his pen to write the introduction:

> Inasmuch as we are bound by the admonition of the Divine Word to administer our office and government . . . above all to constantly admonish and lead our subjects to devout knowledge and fear of the Almighty and His work of salvation . . . we have secured the preparation of a summary course or catechism of our Christian religion, according to the Word of God.

Confrontation at the Diet of Augsburg

Demand for the Heidelberg Catechism was amazing. In 1563, the year of its publication, it went through three editions. Frederick revised certain points, wanting to make still clearer the idolatrous nature of the Mass. Outside the Palatinate, people were taking sides. Zwinglians and Calvinists generally approved of the catechism. Predictably, the Roman Catholic princes and their bishops were against it and began to circulate rumors about its authors: Olevianus was possessed by the devil; Frederick was not able to sleep at night because the devil bothered him. The strongest opponents of the catechism, however, were the High Lutherans, led by Tilemann Hesshus and Duke Christopher of Württemberg.

Duke Christopher challenged Frederick to a debate in April of 1564. Ursinus led eight scholars against eight of the Duke's theologians. They began with the question, "Is the body of Christ in all places?" After three days on this question, Frederick was still willing to say, "I am not yet tired of the debate, for I came here to learn and I still want to learn my whole life long." Seven days later, no progress had been made and both sides went home. Christopher wrote to Emperor Maximilian II, accusing Frederick of abandoning the tenets of the Augsburg Confession. For the sake of the empire, Christopher felt Frederick should be expelled.

Maximilian II was a moderate Catholic, but his rule depended on firm control over the Protestant princes. He feared that escalation of the conflict might lead to civil war. The matter needed to be cleared up, and dispensing with Frederick would be the obvious solution. Yet irritating as Frederick's theology was, his courage and piety were hard to ignore. Maximilian decided to give Frederick one more chance. He ordered the elector to appear in Augsburg to defend his position.

Frederick was well aware of the danger he faced. His friends feared that he would not return alive. But his faith was strong. "There may be danger in store for me at the Diet," he told them, "but I have a comforting hope and trust in my heavenly Father, that he will make me an instrument for his own power . . . not in word only, but also in deed and truth."

By the time Frederick arrived in Augsburg, no one held much hope for him. The High Lutherans had lobbied effectively, and even the few who supported him in principle dared not say so openly. Only Augustus of Saxony publicly defended him.

On May 14, 1566, the charges were read. Frederick was accused of heresy and required to turn from the Reformed faith on penalty of banishment. He found strength as the first question of his beloved catechism echoed in his mind: "What is your only comfort, in life and in death?" And the answer came: "That I belong—body and soul, in life and in death—not to myself but to my faithful Savior, Jesus Christ." All were quiet as Frederick patiently explained the purpose and principles of the catechism he had sponsored. He remained calm and confident. Even his enemies were impressed.

Unexpectedly, the more moderate Lutheran princes petitioned the emperor not to censor or punish Frederick. Maximilian listened. He too had been impressed with Frederick's unfailing kindness and calmness. Aware of powerful support for Frederick's position from Heinrich Bullinger and other Reformed Protestants in Switzerland, Maximilian accepted the petition. Frederick was acquitted of all charges. The catechism had passed its most difficult test because its peaceful and courageous spirit had pervaded the person of its sponsor. Emperor Maximilian nicknamed the Palatinate elector Frederick the Pious.

Essential Tenets of the Reformed Faith

Stewardship

The Book of Order lists, as one of the distinctive tenets, or beliefs, of the Reformed tradition, "A faithful stewardship that shuns ostentation and seeks proper use of the gifts of God's creation." Stewardship, in the Reformed tradition, is not a fancy word for giving money. It means, rather, an attitude toward all of life. God alone is the creator. We are creatures given a special mandate as stewards, or servants, to care for all that God has made. The doctrine of creation comes from Genesis 1. Stewardship derives from Genesis 2. And sin is found in Genesis 3.

The Heidelberg Catechism is structured to deal with the three principal themes of the Christian life: Sin, Redemption, and Thankfulness. These themes have sometimes been stated in more memorable form as Guilt, Grace, and Gratitude, or Sin, Salvation, and Service. A distinctive character of the Reformed faith is revealed in the order or sequence of these themes. The distinction can best be explained by discussing the role of the Ten Commandments in the Christian life.

From the time of the sixteenth-century Reformation, three uses of the Law, or the Ten Commandments, have been suggested. The first use is to convict us of our sins. The second is to help keep public order. The third is to guide and encourage Christians in righteous living.

The first use of the Law was stressed by Luther. In a Lutheran worship service one may expect to hear the Ten Commandments read sometime before the sermon. The Law, for Luther, was to bring us to conviction of our sins so that we would be ready to hear the gospel of forgiveness.

The second use of the Law has been a part of the civil religion of most Western nations. Many secular people have been glad to stress the value of the Ten Commandments as an aid to maintaining a peaceful and well-ordered society.

Only the Reformed have stressed the third use of the Law. We have been elected, chosen by God in sheer grace and mercy. We do not have to earn our salvation. It is a free gift. Of what use, then, is the Law? It gives us a pattern by which to show our gratitude for grace. The Ten Commandments are not only impossible burdens for sinners to keep, they are an indelible pattern for the Christian life of joy and thankfulness. In a Reformed worship service, the Ten Commandments should probably come after the sermon, certainly after the Assurance of Pardon. The Heidelberg Catechism makes this message clear even by the medium of where its discussion of the Ten Commandments and Prayer are placed. They come at the end, in the section on gratitude.

Stewardship of all of life and God's creation is a Reformed expression of our gratitude to God for our creation and redemption. In medieval Catholicism, there were two classes of people religiously: the "secular" and the "religious." Even within the clergy there was a division. Regular priests were called "secular" priests. The "religious" were the ordained monks (along with lay brothers and nuns in religious orders), who were to live according to the "counsel of perfection." They alone were fully called and at least partially able to live according to the full demands of the gospel.

Reformed theology contends that all Christians are on the same plane. We are all sinners, saved by grace. We all have access to the same resources of Word, sacrament, and prayer. We are all called to live, in the power of the Spirit, the same life to which only monks and nuns were called in the Middle Ages. Reformed Christians believe that, as those given the greatest of all gifts, salvation, we should respond by living a simple, disciplined life, being good stewards of all that God has given us.

Stewardship is not just a matter of what to pledge in the annual fund-raising campaign. For Reformed Christians in the Presbyterian Church, stewardship is an attitude toward life. We are saved to serve. Grace motivates us to live in gratitude. Redemption calls us to respond in thankfulness by caring for all of God's creation and all of God's creatures.

The Sacrament of the Lord's Supper

The word "sacrament" does not appear in the Bible. It comes from a Latin word, *sacramentum,* which denoted a military oath taken by Roman soldiers, by which they pledged allegiance to their commanders and promised not to desert their flag.

The word "sacrament," in this sense of a life-and-death commitment, was first used in the church for Baptism. During the first centuries of the church, it was applied to a large and indefinite number of ceremonies. By the Middle Ages it was standardized to refer to seven rites: Baptism, confirmation, the Eucharist, penance, extreme unction (last rites at death), holy orders, and marriage. It would appear that at each critical stage in a person's development, and in each week, there were sacraments meant to infuse God's grace into persons to strengthen them for their tasks.

The Protestant Reformers argued that biblically there were only two sacraments: Baptism and the Lord's Supper. The primary criterion for selection was that a sacrament had to be instituted by Christ. Further, these two sacraments are distinguished by three factors. Each has an external sign. For Baptism it is water, and for the Lord's Supper, bread and wine. Each points to a particular reality. In Baptism it is the new birth, and in the Lord's Supper it is the presence of Christ. Each is proclaimed in Scripture. The Word of God binds the external sign to the reality which it signifies and makes that reality effective in the life of the believer.

Differing Protestant Views of the Lord's Supper

The theory of medieval Roman Catholicism was that, in the Mass, the substance of the bread and wine was changed into the substance of the body and blood of Jesus Christ. This change, called transubstantiation, did not affect the external appearance, called the "accidents," of the bread and wine. But a transformation took place in the essence, or "substance," of the elements, which became the physical body and blood of Christ. Thus Christ was actually resacrificed for people's sins during the medieval Mass.

It was this resacrificing of Christ to which the Protestant Reformers strenuously objected. They were in agreement that Christ's death on the cross had once and for all paid the penalty for human sin. Christ did not need to be sacrificed again. The grace of God did not need to be infused into people weekly and at critical stages in their life. God's grace in Christ was imputed—granted—to people once and for all when they became Christians.

But Protestants could not agree among themselves on a different theory of the Lord's Supper to replace the explanation of transubstantiation. Lutherans held to a theory that has sometimes been called "consubstantiation." Luther was concerned to assert the physical, bodily presence of Christ in the Lord's Supper. His philosophical view that Christ's body could be ubiquitous, or present everywhere at the same time, made that theory possible. His linguistic view, that Christ's words in this instance had to be taken literally, made a view like consubstantiation necessary for Luther.

Zwingli thought Luther was wrong both philosophically and linguistically. For Zwingli, the philosophical truth was the locality, not ubiquity, of Christ's body. According to Scripture, Christ's resurrected body was in heaven. Objects can only be in one place at a time, and thus Christ's body could not be all over the world occupying the bread and wine of the Lord's Supper. Linguistically, according to Zwingli, Christ's words instituting the Lord's Supper were clearly metaphorical, or symbolic. Jesus was physically there at the Last Supper when he handed bread to his disciples and said "This is my body." He meant, This will symbolize, or stand for, my body when you do this act in remembrance of me. For Zwingli, the Lord's Supper was a memorial, an act of remembering who Christ is and what he has done for us.

Calvin could not agree wholly with either the physical, substantial view of Luther or the memorial, symbolic view of Zwingli. Philosophically and linguistically, Calvin agreed with Zwingli. But Calvin wished to honor and affirm the basic value of the Lutheran and Roman Catholic position—

that Christ was really present in the Lord's Supper and that believers were united with Christ there. Calvin's view was, therefore, that Jesus Christ was really present in the Lord's Supper, not physically but spiritually.

One element contributed to the liturgy of the Lord's Supper by followers of Calvin is called the *sursum corda,* "Lift up your hearts." When the presiding minister says that, the people respond, "We lift them up unto the Lord." As Reformed Christians, we are lifting our hearts up to commune with the risen Christ in heaven. Spiritually, Christ is our host at the Lord's Table, rather than being physically present in the elements.

Contemporary Relevance

Stewardship of Our Environment

Many people believe that we are in an environmental crisis. In the cities we experience air pollution and acid rain. Rural areas see depletion of the once rich soil. All of us are aware of dwindling natural resources. Some responsible experts predict that even if we escape the devastation of nuclear war, by the end of the century we could be faced with catastrophic famine and epidemic disease because of what we have done to our environment.

In the late 1800s a new science appeared called "ecology." The word comes from the Greek *oikos,* meaning house. It is the same Greek root from which we have taken our word "ecumenical," meaning the whole household of God. Actually the whole environment, the creation, is the dwelling place, the household of God. God is the creator both of humans and of our natural environment. A proper relationship is therefore based on a threefold interaction between God, humankind, and nature.

During the past two decades, scholars have sought the roots of our present ecological problems. Sometimes the Christian faith has been blamed. Christianity has been accused of being excessively individualistic and otherworldly. A concern only for people and their fate in heaven has led, so critics have alleged, to an unfeeling exploitation of nature. One result of the separation between humanity and nature has been the rise of modern science and technology. The negative side effects have been our attendant ecological problems.

Christian theologians have responded to these charges by showing that the Bible manifests a Hebraic concern for the whole of life: divine, human, and natural. Biblically, God is immanent, within and involved with the world, as well as transcendent, above and distinct from the world. Calvin wrote that because God "uses all the elements to serve his glory," the earth and stones could bear the character of "sacraments" (*Institutes* IV. xiv. 18).

In Jesus Christ, God entered humanity in this natural world. The promise of redemption in Christ is not only for human beings but for the whole creation (Rom. 8:19–23). God created the world as recorded in Genesis 1, and finally God will make all things new as recorded in Revelation 21:5. Between that beginning and that end, humankind has been entrusted with the task of being stewards, caretakers of God's originally good creation.

The Lord's Supper is a symbol that God works through the elements of nature to bring about redemption and renewal. Ordinary bread and wine become the means of communion with the real spiritual presence of the risen Christ. We are called not just to be nourished by these elements but to become Christian activists in the defense of the world God has created. Christians at the National Episcopal Cathedral in Washington, D.C., have prayed to the God whose earth this is to "guide us to restore to our planet beauty and a sound ecology and to the human family peace, justice, and reconciliation." Presbyterians, for whom stewardship is an essential belief, can wholeheartedly pray that prayer.

Children at the Lord's Table

In recent years, Presbyterians have permitted baptized children to partake of the Lord's Supper at the discretion of their parents. An action of the reuniting General Assembly in 1983 declared, "Children should be welcomed, invited, and encouraged to respond to the invitation of Christ and the church, should be baptized and then welcomed to the Lord's Table." To feel comfortable with this position, Presbyterians need to understand both the purpose and the pedagogy, or style of communication, of the sacrament of Communion. Traditionally, only those who had publicly professed their trust in Christ were invited to the Lord's Table. The recent position involves an expansion of our view of what trust in Christ entails and how it occurs.

The purpose of the Lord's Supper is to bring people into union with Christ. It is not a badge of our conversion but a means to bring us into the real, spiritual presence of Christ. Jesus said, "Unless you turn and become like children, you will never enter the kingdom of heaven" (Matt. 18:3). Children have not merited entrance into the kingdom of God. They can only receive it as a gift. Like children, we all enjoy the same spiritual status. Justification is by grace, given by God.

Even when we remember the purpose of Communion, we sometimes feel that it is appropriate only for those who understand what it means. That is true. But understanding comes in many ways. Not only are there cognitive or intellectual or mental forms, there are visual ways of understanding. There are kinesthetic, or touching, ways of understanding. There are emotional, or feeling, ways of understanding. So there are means of understanding appropriate to the level of children as well as of adults. In the Old Testament, we read that whole families, including children, partook of the Passover, the Hebrew predecessor to the Lord's Supper. In fact, the very *youngest* child, in Jewish practice, has always had a prominent place in the ceremony, asking the questions which lead to the father's explanation of the meaning of the Passover meal.

Presbyterian parents are responsible for helping their children understand the meaning of the Lord's Supper. But parents are not alone in this preparation. At the baptism of each child the members of the congregation promise to aid in the spiritual upbringing of that child.

Churches need to provide experiences which will make not only the Lord's Supper but the worship of God each Sunday more accessible to children. Christian educators have provided both ideas and resources to make worship a truly intergenerational experience, not just an adult one. Jesus said, "Whoever receives one such child in my name receives me; and whoever receives me, receives not me but him who sent me" (Mark 9:37). We need to remember and put into practice what we know—that learning is not just listening but involves our total experience in our environment. The Lord's Supper is a meal which engages our five senses and our whole being. We smell the bread and touch the cup. We taste the food as we see it served and hear the biblical words of invitation. As whole persons we encounter the real, spiritual presence of Christ. Not only children but adults, as real people, may have more meaningful communion with a real God at each time of worship, and especially in the Lord's Supper.

7

The Second Helvetic Confession
A.D. 1566

Least well known of all the creedal documents in our *Book of Confessions* is the Second Helvetic Confession. In the early 1960s, when a book of confessions was first being considered, there was no adequate translation in English of this confession. A new translation, published in 1966 at the time of the 400th anniversary of the Second Helvetic Confession, now provides access to this amazingly contemporary document.

In its own time, the Second Helvetic Confession held the highest authority among the Reformed confessions. It is longer than any of the other Reformed creeds, having thirty chapters. It breathes an ecumenical spirit. In 1581, *The Harmony of Protestant Confessions* used the Second Helvetic Confession as the basis with which other Reformed confessions were correlated to show the consensus among them.

The historical context of the Second Helvetic Confession introduces us to two early Reformers, Ulrich Zwingli and Heinrich Bullinger. They are less well known than Luther and Calvin, but they exerted great influence in their own time and in many countries.

Zwingli was born on January 1, 1484. In 1984, to mark the 500th anniversary of his birth, celebrations were held in Switzerland and elsewhere. Numerous articles were published which have heightened appreciation for this earliest of the sixteenth-century Reformers.

"Before anyone in my neighborhood had even heard Luther's name mentioned," Zwingli wrote, "I began to preach the gospel of Christ in the year 1516." That was one year before Luther posted his ninety-five theses. One reason that Luther's work was better known is that he was a university professor in a major city, calling other theologians to debate current issues. In 1506, Zwingli was a parish priest in the obscure village of Glarus in the Swiss mountains. After ten years there, he spent two years as chaplain at a monastery in Einsiedeln. Zwingli's reforming tendencies only became well known when in 1519 he was called to be the "people's priest" or preaching minister at the cathedral church, the Great Minster, in the city of Zürich. On his thirty-fifth birthday, Zwingli mounted the steps to the high pulpit and announced, "I did not learn Christ's teaching from Luther but from the very word of God." In 1524, Zwingli and other Zürich Reformers published a German New Testament, with the entire Bible in the common language following in 1530. That was four years before Luther's German translation was available.

During Lent in 1522, Zwingli was present when the leader of the printer's union served sausages to his comrades. It was a political act, which some have compared to burning a draft card. Zwingli did not eat the meat himself, but the following Sunday he abolished the Lenten fast, although without condemning the traditionalists: "If you want to fast, do so; if you do not want to eat meat, don't eat it; but allow Christians a free choice."

Earlier, Zwingli had been pressured by influential laity to leave his post in Glarus. In part this was due to his outspoken opposition to the practice of recruiting Swiss peasants as mercenaries, soldiers for hire, by European powers and by the pope himself. Zwingli recognized an unjust system. "Some condemn the eating of meat on Fridays and consider it a great sin, though God has never forbidden it," he declared. "But to sell human flesh—that they do not consider a great sin." Yet this same Zwingli died in full battle armor in an ill-conceived and poorly organized war between citizens of Protestant Zürich and an overwhelming force from the Catholic cantons at Kappel in October 1531.

Zwingli was an accomplished Renaissance scholar. His scholarly study established the authority of the Bible over the church's traditions. Thus he declared, "You must drop all that and learn God's will directly from his own Word." Zwingli loved music and played several instruments. Yet he oversaw not only the whitewashing of church walls but the dismantling of organs. He wanted nothing to distract worshippers from hearing the Word of God. Zwingli believed that Christ was spiritually present, not in the communion bread but in the people who received Christ by faith. The congregation was the body of Christ.

Heinrich Bullinger was twenty years younger than Zwingli, but they were close friends. The volatile Zwingli began a reformation; the pastoral Bullinger solidified and preserved it. After Zwingli's death, Bullinger succeeded him as pastor of the Great Minster in Zürich. Bullinger became chief minister in Zürich in 1531, before Calvin was converted to Protestantism. He continued as a leader of the Reformed community until his death in 1575, eleven years after Calvin's passing. Bullinger was recognized as the senior Reformed theologian and pastor, who in his lifetime saw three generations of Reformers rise up and go to their reward, many of them as martyrs.

Bullinger helped write the First Helvetic Confession, which he hoped would bring reconciliation with the Lutherans. He corresponded widely with other Reformed leaders. His books of sermons, entitled *Decades,* were required reading for English Protestant clergy at one period. The first Dutch preacher in New Amsterdam was ordered by his superiors in Holland to memorize Bullinger's sermons and preach them to his congregation in the New World. Bullinger's influence came to this country as well through his imprint on English Puritanism.

The Second Helvetic Confession was Bullinger's personal testimony. He wrote it after surviving the plague in 1561. He intended that it be attached to his will as a gift to the city of Zürich but published it in 1566 in response to a request for support from fellow Reformed believers in Heidelberg. Now we have the opportunity to benefit from its biblically grounded wisdom.

Historical Context: The Case of the Second Helvetic Confession

Heinrich Bullinger sat in his study near the Great Minster of Zürich, holding a letter in his hand. His eyes scanned the page again. It was signed by the Chancellor to Frederick III, Elector of the Palatinate of Heidelberg. According to the letter, Frederick had been ordered to appear before Emperor Maximilian II in May of this year, 1566. Frederick was charged with "adopting a new catechism not in agreement with the tenets of the Augsburg confession of 1530 . . . promulgating Reform heresy." These were serious charges in Germany, as Bullinger well knew.

In his sixty-two years, Bullinger had seen three generations of Reformers develop—from Melanchthon and the early Lutherans and his own magnetic mentor, Ulrich Zwingli, to Calvin, the scholar and administrator, and the young and fiery Knox. Now two young men barely over twenty years old, Olevianus of Trier and Ursinus, who had gone from Zürich, had written a Heidelberg Catechism for Frederick. What triumph Bullinger had seen in the last forty years, and what desolation! How many, he wondered, had been martyred for the Reformed faith? Hundreds? Perhaps thousands? Would Frederick be another one?

The Roots of Reform

Martin Luther and Ulrich Zwingli had emerged as prime movers of the Reformation within the space of a year. Zwingli had begun his preaching of reform in 1516. Luther gained instant notoriety in 1517 in Wittenberg. From that point on, the two branches of the Reformation grew independently, one in Germany and the other in Switzerland. Each took a different direction theologically and ecclesiastically.

Luther's great emphasis was doctrinal. Scripture alone, grace alone, faith alone were his watchwords. Scripture was the ultimate authority on earth. In 1522, Luther published his first German translation from the Greek New Testament. In 1534 he completed the Old Testament. The timing was right. The newly invented movable-type printing press and a rising tide of literacy combined to make Luther's German Bible a revolutionary document which helped to standardize a common German language.

The Lutherans shied away from advocating social, political, or liturgical reforms, content simply to modify Roman Catholic practices while working within the established ecclesiastical framework. They saw no harm in retaining Catholic liturgy and symbols. Indeed, every practice not specifically prohibited by Scripture was acceptable. The crucifix, vestments, paintings, and relics, as well as some features of the Roman Catholic service of Communion, were all continued in the Lutheran Church.

Zwingli and his Swiss followers were less tolerant of the Roman Catholic Church and more militant in their approach to reform. They retained nothing of Catholic practice except those acts specifically commanded by Scripture. Simple to the point of austerity, their churches were stripped of crucifixes and "popish decorations."

Zwingli wanted nothing less than a complete overhaul of all facets of church life. Yet he did not overtly organize reform. He simply preached from Scripture and allowed the demand for reformation to emerge from the people. For Zwingli, the preached word and God's Word were identical. God's Word was clear and understandable; no "expert" interpreters were needed. The results of his innovative and powerful preaching in Zürich were startling. By 1524, distracting objects such as organs, statues, and paintings had been removed from the church. Processions, festivals (except Christmas and Easter), saint's days, and numerous other medieval practices gradually were abolished. The local monastery was dissolved and the monks dispersed. In 1525, the City Council banned the Catholic Eucharist, replacing it with a radically simplified "service of communion" in which the elements were distributed in the pews instead of at the altar. A sermon was substituted for the Mass. The church service was given in German, not Latin.

Ulrich Zwingli's radical emphasis on the clarity of Scripture had more than one result: laypeople, for example, began to study the Bible and to express their own beliefs. Weekly Bible study groups sprouted in homes in and around Zürich. Before long, some of these groups began to feel that Zwingli's reforms did not go quite far enough. They wanted to return to what they believed to be the primitive simplicity of the first-century church as described in the New Testament. For them, Old Testament beliefs and practices paled in the light of the New Covenant with Jesus Christ. They felt that true reform could be found only in the total rejection of all post-Scriptural church tradition and the full reinstatement of New Testament doctrine and life-style.

These reformers of the Reformed church were called Anabaptists, or "re-baptizers." They discounted infant baptism and practiced only adult baptism of believers, modeled after what they held to be the New Testament example. In so doing, they sparked controversy and evoked a persecution throughout Europe that altered the course of the Reformation.

Anabaptists: The Radical Reformers

The name Anabaptists was given to many loosely organized, highly varied groups. Their leaders were scholars, cobblers, ex-priests, mystics, and monks. They attracted dissatisfied evangelicals and radical revolutionaries. Three main-line Anabaptist offshoots were the Hutterites, who lived communally in Moravia, the pacifistic Mennonites in the Netherlands, and the Swiss Brethren in Zürich. This last group began to criticize Zwingli in 1525 for his adherence to the sacrament of infant baptism.

In a defiant gesture, Swiss Anabaptist leaders Conrad Grebel, Felix Manz, and Balthasar Hubmaier baptized their friend George Blaurock on January 21, 1525. In March, the town council of Zürich declared that anyone baptized as an adult would be executed without benefit of trial. Manz was the first victim, followed by Hubmaier in 1528 and Blaurock in 1529. Anabaptists were seen as anarchists bent on the destruction of society and were persecuted with terrible ferocity. By the early 1520s, hundreds of Anabaptists had been drowned, beheaded, or burned.

For most Anabaptists, the simplicity, disciplined behavior, and strict morality of the Sermon on the Mount were possible achievements where personal faith was voluntary and was nurtured in a "gathered" community of believers separated from the impurity of the world. The belief that the church was a covenant community constituted by voluntary agreement among believing adults was central in their doctrine. Since infants did not yet have faith and could not enter into such an agreement, they were not considered eligible for baptism.

Unlike Old Testament circumcision—a sacrament administered to infants—baptism could occur only when faith was already present. Before his death, Conrad Grebel wrote to fellow Anabaptist Thomas Müntzer:

> We hold . . . that all children who have not yet come to . . . the knowledge of good and evil . . . are surely saved

> by the suffering of Christ, the New Adam. . . . But as to the objection that faith is demanded of all who are to be saved, we exclude children from this and hold that they are saved without faith, and we do not believe . . . [children must be baptized], and we conclude from [the Bible] (according to which no child was baptized), that infant baptism is a senseless, blasphemous abomination, contrary to all Scripture, contrary even to the papacy.

As far as the Anabaptists were concerned, their name was incorrect. Infant baptism was no baptism at all. They were not "re-baptizing" adults but baptizing them for the first time. In the Schleitheim Articles (1527), the only doctrinal statement recorded by early Anabaptists, they called infant baptism "the highest and chief abomination of the pope." In the same document they proclaimed the righteousness of adult baptism and separation from the world, banned attendance at parish churches and taverns, and forbade the use of force, the taking of oaths, and careers in law. The church was to have nothing to do with the state, and the state should have no right of jurisdiction over the church.

Disaster at Münster

Near the end of 1533, the Anabaptist faction at Münster in Westphalia, under the leadership of former Lutheran Bernt Rothmann, gained control of the town council. A few months later, a self-styled Dutch prophet and ex-innkeeper, John Van Leyden, appeared in town, announcing that God had appointed him to make the city a New Jerusalem. On February 9, 1534, his followers seized City Hall. On March 2, the order was issued that all who refused adult baptism would be banished. At the same time, the city was officially declared a haven for the oppressed. Van Leyden proclaimed himself king, set up his throne in the market square, and sported royal robes. New laws were passed mandating a community of goods, and the Old

Testament was cited to permit polygamy. Rothmann, once the sensible friend of Philip Melanchthon, took nine wives.

The Münsterites believed that the end of the age was near and that it was their duty to kill the ungodly. Van Leyden dreamed that the entire world would be destroyed; only Münster would survive. In May of 1535, thirty Münsterites attacked the city hall in Amsterdam, killing the mayor and several citizens. Other Anabaptists ran naked through the streets, announcing the end of the world. Finally, the Roman Catholic bishop's army entered the city, killed every Anabaptist leader, and displayed their bodies in iron cages. This was meant as an unpleasant object lesson to any others considering joining the revolt.

The Münster incident irreparably damaged the cause of the many Anabaptists who were quiet and nonviolent. It also limited the credibility of anyone who spoke out for religious toleration. Furthermore, it cast a shadow over the Reformed movement, because of the early relationship between Zwingli and the Swiss Brethren, and tended to solidify the attitude of Lutherans and Roman Catholics against the "Reform heresy."

Zwingli and the Covenant Controversy

The doctrine of Baptism held an important position in Zwingli's theology, particularly after the rise of the Anabaptists in Zürich. Many early Anabaptists had championed Zwingli's Reformed cause. He, in turn, was at first impressed by their direct appeal to Scripture and their uncompromising attitude, but by 1525 he had changed his view. Thereafter he strongly encouraged Reformed Christians to stand firm against the "new error." Anabaptists under Grebel retaliated with demonstrations, shouting that they wanted "the Word of God, not the word of Zwingli." Hubmaier jumped into the fray with a tract called *The Christian Baptism of Believers.* Zwingli countered with *A Refutation of the Tricks of the Anabaptists* (1531).

Zwingli agreed with the Anabaptists that the church was a covenant community. But for him the primary covenant was the one God made with Adam and renewed for all time with Abraham. Throughout history, no matter how many times it was restated or renewed, the covenant was still the same. The appearance of Jesus Christ was not its beginning but its fulfillment, he said. Further, the church since the time of Jesus was still guided by that same covenant. There was no chasm between the covenant of the Old Testament and that of the New Testament. Despite certain outward changes, the history of the people of God was unified and continuous.

Zwingli cited circumcision and baptism as parallels. Infants were included in the covenant through circumcision before they believed. It was right, therefore, for the children of Christian believers to be included in the church through the sacrament of infant baptism before they believed. Zwingli held that the covenant sign belonged to families, not just to individual adults. The real reason for infant baptism was not to signify human willingness to accept God's service; it was to signify God's willingness to accept people as his servants.

Heinrich Bullinger and the Helvetic Confessions

Zwingli was killed, sword in hand, when the Protestants were routed at the Battle of Kappel in 1531. His death left Reformed Christians without a leader and the pulpit of the great cathedral in Zürich without a preacher. The Council of Zürich chose as Zwingli's successor his younger friend and colleague, Heinrich Bullinger.

Bullinger was born in 1504 to a German priest and his common-law wife. He studied at Cologne. Although the university emphasized medieval Scholasticism, the young scholar was soon attracted to the works of early church theologians: Ambrose, Augustine, Origen, and Chrysostom. Then he discovered Luther and Melanchthon, who seemed to him to be more in harmony with the Bible and the early church theologians than were the Roman Catholics. Bullinger had planned to join a Carthusian monastery, but he converted to Protestantism in 1522. He agreed to teach the Bible as a lay professor in a Cistercian cloister. So powerful was his teaching that four years later the monastery was dissolved and converted to a Protestant church with Bullinger as its pastor.

Bullinger met Zwingli in 1523. Although Zwingli was twenty years older, the two became fast friends. Bullinger's serious academic nature seemed the ideal complement to Zwingli's meteoric personality. After Zwingli's death, Bullinger fled to Zürich, where he was appointed chief minister of the cathedral church. He rallied Swiss Protestants, infused new life into the dejected followers of Zwingli, and sparked unparalleled growth in the church. Bullinger's books of collected sermons, *Decades,* influenced all of Europe. He was considered a wise and compassionate counselor as well as a brilliant and prolific writer.

In 1536, Bullinger met with a handful of Swiss colleagues to write a confession with the purpose of unifying the German Lutheran and Swiss Reformed against the Roman Catholic Counter-Reformation. Luther eventually rejected this First Helvetic (Swiss) Confession. It did, however, serve to unify all of German-speaking Switzerland and paved the way for Bullinger's personal confession of 1561.

Bullinger wrote the Second Helvetic Confession entirely on his own. It was the outgrowth of his forty years of experience as chief minister in Zürich. The confession was structured in thirty chapters, divided between two major sections: the first on theology and the second on the church, ministry, and sacraments. A lengthy document, it was nevertheless written in simple language with an eye to practical application in daily life. Ever hopeful of reconciliation between German Lutheran and Swiss Reformed churches, Bullinger stressed the wholeness and oneness of the church.

Chapters I through XVI dealt with Scripture and preaching, true worship, creation, sin, the work of salvation, and new life. The early church theologians, particularly Augustine, were frequently cited. This was the first document of its kind to set forth formal guidelines for the interpretation of Scripture:

> The apostle Peter has said that the Holy Scriptures are not of private interpretation (II Peter 1:20), and thus we do not allow all possible interpretations. Nor consequently do we acknowledge as the true or genuine interpretation of the Scriptures what . . . the defenders of the Roman Church plainly maintain should be thrust upon all for acceptance. But we hold that interpretation of the Scripture to be orthodox and genuine which is gleaned from the Scriptures themselves (from the nature of the language in which they were written . . . the circumstances in which they were set down, and expounded in the light of like and unlike passages and of many and clearer passages). (Chapter II)

Chapters XVII through XXX were a full exposition of the practical aspects of the church and the ministry. The church was described as "an assembly of the faithful . . . Citizens of One Commonwealth." Ministers were "God's stewards," whose primary duties were to preach the Gospel of Christ and to administer the sacraments properly.

The sacraments were "mystical symbols" instituted by God which serve to remind believers of God's goodness. God used them to seal his promises, strengthen faith, designate the true religion, and bind believers to himself. Bullinger gave an entire chapter (XX) to the sacrament of Baptism, the "enrollment" into God's covenant, leaving no doubt concerning his views of the Anabaptists and adult baptism:

> We condemn the Anabaptists, who deny that newborn infants of the faithful are to be baptized. For according to evangelical teaching, of such is the Kingdom of God,

> and they are in the covenant of God. Why, then, should the sign of God's covenant not be given to them? Why should those who belong to God and are in his Church not be initiated by holy baptism? We condemn also the Anabaptists in the rest of their peculiar doctrines which they hold contrary to the Word of God. We therefore are not Anabaptists and have nothing in common with them.

Bullinger followed this with several chapters outlining church practices, such as private prayers (to be poured out to God alone, through Christ), public prayers (not to be "excessively long and irksome"), singing (in moderation, and not the Gregorian Chant, which "has many foolish things in it"), holy days ("we do not approve of feasts instituted for men and for saints"), fasting (which is not the same as stuffing the stomach once a day and abstaining from food at a certain prescribed time, "thinking that by having done this work [we] please God"), youth (to be instructed in godliness), and the sick (to be visited and comforted as well as prayed for).

The Confession concluded with practical concerns, capped by a full and sympathetic treatment of family life, establishing marriage as "instituted by the Lord God himself." One of Bullinger's most innovative ideas was the "Matrimonial Forum," a unique counseling center and court for helping and making decisions about troubled marriages. Children were to be brought up in the fear of the Lord, taught "honest trades or professions," and kept from idleness, "lest through a lack of confidence or too much security or filthy greed they become dissolute and achieve no success." The confession ended with a declaration on the Christian state, whose purpose it was to guard and nurture the church, secure peace, and preserve public tranquillity for its citizens, subject to the Law of God.

The Request from Heidelberg

Heinrich Bullinger weighed the issues raised by the letter before him. Was it possible to reconcile the High Lutheran and Reformed movements? If he were to send his personal confession to Frederick, would it have a conciliatory effect or would it only aggravate the opposition? Perhaps he should stick to his original plan: attach this confession to his will and draft a more moderate statement that might placate Maximilian. There was no one to ask: Zwingli, Peter Martyr, Melanchthon, Calvin . . . all were dead. Bullinger felt alone.

High in the cathedral a bell tolled the hour. Time was passing. Frederick's life might depend on Bullinger's decision. The aged pastor prayed and then came to a decision. There was no time to write another statement. This one would have to do. It represented Bullinger's reflections on a lifetime of ministry. He could only hope that it would encourage Frederick and show the emperor that Frederick was not peculiar in his views. The Reformed movement sought only to be faithfully biblical and in harmony with the whole Christian church.

Essential Tenets of the Reformed Faith

Covenant

One doctrine which may serve to focus on the distinctively Reformed contribution to ecumenical Christianity is *covenant.* The concept of covenant sums up much of what being Reformed is all about. Although it is not specifically mentioned in the Second Helvetic Confession, Bullinger emphasized it in his theology, as can be seen in *Decades,* his published sermons. The subject is treated here because the historical context of Zwingli's and Bullinger's ministries raised the issue of differing views of covenant. The argument with the Anabaptists forced a clarification of many concerns which were and are part of the Reformed consciousness.

For Reformed Christians, there is just one covenant in the Bible. God has not and does not change in character, attitude toward people, or purpose for the world. God did not, for example, offer salvation through keeping the law to the people of the Old Testament and then, when that didn't work well, change and offer salvation by grace to people in the New Testament dispensation. Reformed people believe that God is and has always been a God of grace.

This covenant of grace in the Bible has appeared in many forms. The original covenant, according to Reformed thinking, was made by God with Adam and Eve in the Garden of Eden. Then God made a covenant with Noah before the flood that he would spare Noah and his family. After the flood, God renewed the covenant with Noah and all living creatures that he would never again destroy the world in this way. God made a covenant with Abraham and his descendants with promises of land and blessing, using the rite of circumcision as a sign of identity. God made a covenant with Moses, which is a good instance of the fact that God's mercy precedes the law, because God had already brought the children of Israel out of slavery in Egypt. Then God gave them the law. Its function was not to earn God's favor but to show God's covenant people how to live the most wholesome and worthwhile style of life. And God made a covenant with David and promised that from David's family ultimately would come the Messiah, a redeemer, for all people.

When the prophet Jeremiah announced a new covenant, it was not a covenant new in content but new in its form and application. One day, Jeremiah declared, everyone would know this covenant, and it would be written on the hearts of all people that God is their God and they are God's people. This covenant theme is celebrated and reinforced every time we celebrate the Lord's Supper. The wine reminds us of the new covenant in Christ's blood, a costly sacrifice on God's part to bring us together as his community.

The themes of this continuous covenant are clear. God established community between God and us, and that creates a community among us. The purpose is peacemaking; human beings should be reconciled to God and to each other. Finally, we should extend this reconciliation, and the results of this reconciling community, to all people.

The Three C's of Presbyterianism

We Presbyterians have had our own particular way of working out the consequences of being a covenant community of God's people. Sometimes we have used "three C's" to express that understanding. We talk about Confession, Constitution, and Connection.

Presbyterians are a covenant people who make confession of their faith. That is why we have a *Book of Confessions.* We Presbyterians believe in doctrine. The book you are now reading is an attempt to help you enter the world of Presbyterian doctrine. All our doctrines center in the person and work of Jesus Christ. We studied that doctrine in chapter 3 on the Nicene Creed. That makes us catholic, or simply Christian. Believing that Jesus Christ is central unites us with all other Christians, because this is the distinctive doctrine of the Christian faith.

Second, Presbyterians are a covenant people who live out their faith according to a constitution. That is why we have a *Book of Order.* Presbyterians believe in order. Decency and order is a Presbyterian slogan we may laugh about, but we value it in practice. In a day of demagogues who appoint themselves leaders and lead people astray, to sit through a boring committee meeting can be a prophetic witness.

Presbyterians as a covenant people believe in corporate decision making. We believe in an orderly representative process. We don't turn our decisions over to some authority figure and say, Here, make our decisions for us. Nor, on the other hand, do we say that we have to be personally involved in every decision. The middle ground we have chosen is a representative process whereby we elect leaders who then act according to their own consciences. This process, like the covenant in Scripture, has privileges and carries accountability and responsibility. This commitment to a constitutional process of government is part of what makes us Reformed.

Third, Presbyterians are a covenant people who act out their faith connectionally. We believe in mission. We believe in sharing the good news and doing good deeds, not just locally but on a world scale. Our being connected with other congregations through our governing bodies enables us to serve in more ways than we could manage by ourselves. For example, we can send fraternal workers to other countries to work with the churches there. We can share with other Christians in bringing disaster relief in emergencies very quickly. And we can share with other Christians in protesting injustice and working to bring about greater love and justice in society. These concerns make us evangelical. We have good news, and we want to share it with all people. The purpose of the covenant is to share its blessings. We have been saved not to hold onto the good news selfishly but to share it in speech and in service.

As Presbyterians we believe ourselves to be members of a covenant community. That covenant centers in Christ, it creates community, and it calls for change. And we are called as a covenant people to a particularly Presbyterian form of acting out that covenant obligation. We declare our faith in confessions. We live according to a constitution. And we help one another to serve connectionally. That does not mean withdrawing into some kind of narrow Presbyterian ghetto. Rather, it is our particular way of acknowledging our oneness with other Christians: that we are catholic, that we are Reformed, and that we are evangelical.

The Sacrament of Baptism

What difference does it make when and how one is baptized? Surely the more important issue is that one *is* baptized as a sign of entrance into the Christian community, either as an infant or as an adult, and either by sprinkling, pouring, or immersion. The differences among Christians regarding Baptism sometimes mask the common concerns which we share.

All Christians believe that Baptism is the biblically required sign of incorporation into the Christian community. All Christians also believe that the children of believing parents are somehow a special part of the Christian community and should be recognized as such. Those who do not baptize infants therefore have a *dedication* of them. All Christians also believe that when children grow to the age of adult responsibility they should make their own personal and public confession of faith. Those who have already baptized children have a time of what has been called *confirmation* of their faith when those children reach the age of accountability.

Christians share the same commitment to Baptism. And they recognize the same needs: to provide for the incorporation of infants into the community and to bring all persons to a time of personal and public confession of faith. The emphases differ because of other values deeply held.

In recent years there has been a renewed interest, within the Reformed tradition, in the option of allowing covenant children to wait until they could make their own public profession of faith and then be baptized. The Swiss theologians Barth and Brunner both advocated this position. It was also a permissible option in the French Reformed Church and The United Presbyterian Church in the U.S.A.

Since the 1983 reunion to form the Presbyterian Church (U.S.A.) there has been greater stress on the values inherent in the baptism of infants. The General Assembly of the Presbyterian Church (U.S.A.), in 1984, received for study proposed revisions of the chapter on baptism for a new directory for worship. These revisions stress the nature of the covenant community, which includes all people, children as well as adults: "So, baptism is the sign of God's grace and covenant in Christ. Just as circumcision is the sign of God's grace and covenant with Israel (Gen. 17:7–14), so baptism is the sign of inclusion in God's grace and covenant with the church."

In Reformed thinking, baptism signifies God's gracious act of bringing us into the covenant community rather than our act of responding in faith. Therefore, baptism is to be received only once. As the report says, "The efficacy of baptism is not tied to the moment when it is administered, for baptism signifies the beginning of the life in Christ, not its completion."

Presbyterians recognize that "our faithfulness to God needs repeated renewal." But there are many times and many ways in which that can be recognized in worship. One special way in which that is done is at a time of making public profession of faith. The new report provides for this need, saying: "When persons baptized as children reach an appropriate age, the session shall invite, encourage, and help them to make public their personal profession of faith in Jesus Christ and to prepare for assuming responsibility for the governance and decision-making of the congregation." After the session has examined people and they have made public profession of faith in worship, they shall be "recognized and commissioned" during a worship service.

The communal nature of the experience of baptism and its interrelations with all of Christian worship and practice are emphasized by the stress that baptism should take place in a service of congregational worship which is "preceded by the reading and preaching of the Word and followed by the celebration of the Lord's Supper." A further recognition of the wholeness of the covenant community is that baptized children are welcomed and encouraged to take part in the Lord's Supper "in ways appropriate to their age and understanding."

It is recommended that the prayer at the time of baptism "shall express thanksgiving for God's covenant faithfulness and shall give praise for God's reconciling acts." The emphasis throughout the Reformed understanding of baptism is on what God does, not on what we do. It further stresses the fact that we belong to a community rather than that we are isolated individuals in our relationship to God. These are not the only values which Christians hold. But they are particular values which are important to Reformed Christians and which are part of our contribution to the richness of the ecumenical fellowship.

Contemporary Relevance

Accountability to the Community

The doctrine of covenant raises important questions about the relationship between the individual and the community. In the Presbyterian system of church government, based on the doctrine of the covenant, questions arise about the rights of the local congregation in relationship to the responsibilities of the denomination as a whole. These questions take on special poignancy at a time when a congregation decides that it must separate from the denomination. As in a divorce between husband and wife, there can be special trauma over the issue of who owns the property.

For the past century Presbyterians had followed the decision of the U.S. Supreme Court in *Watson v. Jones* (1872), which stated, "In a connectional church such as the Presbyterian Church, every local congregation holds all its property in an implied trust for the entire denomination." But confidence in that principle of "implied trust" was challenged in a new decision of the U.S. Supreme Court in the case of *Jones v. Wolf* (1979).

In this case a Presbyterian congregation had voted 164 to 94 to separate itself from the former Presbyterian Church in the U.S. and to unite with another newly established denomination. The Georgia courts decided that the property was owned by the congregation and controlled by a majority vote of its members. The minority of the congregation, supported by the presbytery, had unsuccessfully maintained that the property was held by the congregation in trust for the denomination. The Supreme Court in a 5–4 decision argued that since the Constitution of the Presbyterian Church did not specifically state that all local church property is held in trust for the denomination as a whole, the state may follow "neutral principles of law" in determining ownership of the property of a particular church. In response to this decision, the two Presbyterian denominations which united in 1983 to form the Presbyterian Church (U.S.A.) passed new legislation to state specifically in the Constitution of the church that all property of a particular church is held in trust for the use and benefit of the denomination as a whole.

Deeply felt, but differing, theological and moral principles are called forth from Presbyterians by the property issue. On the one hand, some feel that the pastoral leaders of the church should be concerned solely with the spiritual needs of the people. All temporal matters, such as property, should be left to lay leaders of the local congregation. A related value, held by people taking this view, is that the local congregation is the primary church. Any move to increase the power of higher governing bodies—the presbytery, the synod, or the General Assembly—is a move toward an unacceptable hierarchicalism.

Other Presbyterians argue that it is biblically and theologically unsound to separate the spiritual and material functions of the church. Pastors and elected lay leaders share in a total concern for the total well-being of the people of God. And, these people contend, in a Presbyterian system the local congregation is not primary. Presbyterianism, by its nature and in its organization in this country, displays an organic unity of four levels of governing bodies: session, presbytery, synod, and General Assembly. One of the chief reasons for the organization of the first presbytery in 1706 was the need for a governing body competent to ordain ministers and to organize congregations. Authority and responsibility in this system go both up and down, but effective action usually requires the consent of more than one governing body. In this way, a degree of local autonomy is combined with strong national unity.

Theologically, two different views of the covenant are evidenced in these disputes. In the historical context of the Second Helvetic Confession, it would appear that one more nearly resembles the Anabaptist view. For the Anabaptists, the covenant was a contractual agreement between voluntarily consenting adults. It placed a high premium on individual rights and yielded an emphasis on the autonomy of the local congregation. For the Reformed, the covenant was not created by the contracting parties but by God. All participants in the covenant were chosen by God and thus became part of an organic unity, the body of Christ. The needs of the body hold focus rather than the rights of the individuals. Authority and responsibility reside not just in the local congregation but in the whole body, or denomination. Since in our contemporary mobile society a large percentage of the members of every local congregation come from other than Reformed backgrounds, we need to teach the values of the organic concept of the church that is integral to the Reformed tradition.

Rebaptism and Dedication

One might expect the views and practices of contemporary Presbyterians regarding baptism to be highly diverse in our pluralistic religious culture. A survey conducted by the research agency of the former United Presbyterian Church and published in spring 1983 gave statistical support to that assumption. Thirty-one percent of the pastors surveyed said that they rebaptize persons who request it—despite the fact that in most Christian traditions Baptism is a sacrament to be performed only once. Presbyterians recognize the validity of baptisms performed by any Christian church. Accompanying this stress on the baptism of adult believers is an accompanying pressure on pastors to provide a service of dedication for infants not baptized—despite the fact that there is no provision in the Reformed tradition for such an act.

Presbyterians, like others in our culture, are influenced by a wide variety of religious customs. Increasingly, young people, and often their elders, find religious awakening and renewal not in the church of their baptism but through other denominations, para-church agencies, small groups, and committed friends. We can only be thankful when people respond to God's call in whatever setting. One result, however, is a diminished awareness of the values of the Reformed tradition in its Presbyterian expression. Presbyterians have always been strongly ecumenical, recognizing the validity of other expressions of the Christian faith. Any attempt to assert the particular emphases of Presbyterianism is not intended as a move toward exclusivity but, rather, as an attempt to preserve dimensions of Christian expression and practice which have proved useful in the past.

The current stress on believers' baptism often is the manifestation of a cultural and theological orientation different from that of the Reformed tradition. While, at present, different traditions are rarely mutually exclusive and are often not consciously followed, it might be useful to suggest contrasting lists of attitudes sometimes held by the adherents of believers' baptism as opposed to those held by adherents of infant baptism. Use these contrasting images not as careful definitons but as suggestions to stimulate reflection on your own experience.

BELIEVERS' BAPTISM	*INFANT BAPTISM*
Individual rights	Representative government
Personal piety	Societal transformation
Crisis conversion	Christian nurture
Charismatic leadership	Committee process
Local congregation	Connectional church
Para-church movements	Institutional church
Voluntary contract	Organic union
New Testament replaces Old	Unity of the Bible

These contrasting images suggest that debates between the Anabaptists and the Reformed still go on, even within the American Presbyterian Church.

8

The Westminster Confession of Faith and Catechisms *A.D. 1647*

The Westminster Confession of Faith and the Westminster Larger and Shorter Catechisms are the best known of the Reformation era creeds among Presbyterians. For over three centuries they were the sole doctrinal standards of British and American Presbyterianism. This exclusively Anglo-Saxon and seventeenth-century base was broadened to include ancient creeds, sixteenth- and twentieth-century confessions, and the Swiss and German Reformed theological heritage with the adoption of *The Book of Confessions* by the United Presbyterian Church in 1967 and its inclusion in the Articles of Agreement of the reunion which formed the Presbyterian Church (U.S.A.) in 1983.

The Westminster Confession and Catechisms had a pervasive influence on the theology of early America. Presbyterians, in the Adopting Act of 1729, required ministers to subscribe to the Westminster Confession of Faith "as being in all the essential and necessary articles, good forms of sound words and systems of Christian doctrine." Long before that, other influential Protestant bodies had accepted the theology of the Westminster Confession. In 1648 the Congregational Synod of the Massachusetts Bay Colony adopted the Westminster Confession of Faith, modified to affirm Congregational church polity. Congregational acceptance was broadened in 1708 when the Westminster Confession with Congregational adaptations was accepted by the churches of Connecticut at the Synod of Saybrook.

In 1707, the Philadelphia Confession of Faith, which was the Westminster Confession of Faith modified to embody congregational polity and adult believers' baptism, was adopted by American Baptists; this formed the basis of the Baptist Confession of 1742. The number of children who received their primary religious instruction from the Westminster Shorter Catechism may number in the millions.

The Americanization of the Westminster standards has proved to be a mixed blessing. Isolated from constant interaction with other Reformed confessions and catechisms, they easily took on a peculiarly American interpretation. This was especially true during the period between 1893 and 1927, when the interpretation of the Westminster Confession developed by theologians at Princeton Theological Seminary was declared normative by repeated statements of the General Assembly. One result was that after 1927 few people studied the Westminster Confession. Either they adhered to it, assuming the Old Princeton interpretation, or they ignored it, again assuming the Old Princeton interpretation. Only recent study and action by the church has reopened the question of the validity of this peculiarly American interpretation of these standards.

Since the issue of the appropriate interpretation of the Westminster Confession decisively affects the doctrines we will be examining, particularly the doctrine of Scripture, a thumbnail sketch of the historical problem is needed.

The sixteenth-century Reformers reacted against the repetitiveness and rigidity of medieval Scholasticism. A "scholastic" was a schoolteacher, and Scholasticism came to refer to the teaching of the medieval schools. While it is hard to define, the negative characteristic of Scholasticism was its tendency to reduce theology to a cut-and-dried, logically developed system, which was repeated in textbook after textbook. The Reformers sought to get behind this accumulation of textbook repetition to a fresh examination of the original sources of the Christian faith in Scripture and the teaching of the early church.

In the century following the Protestant Reformation, the Roman Catholic Church consolidated its strength in a Counter-Reformation. Rationalist movements, which led to Unitarianism, were also gaining a hearing. Literary criticism of documents, including the Bible, was rising. In response to these challenges, the Protestant Reformers of the seventeenth century on the European continent took on the methods of their opponents. They developed a Post-Reformation Protestant Scholasticism characterized by the attempt to systematize all Protestant thought and prove the truth of their propositions by human reason and evidence from the natural world.

Reformed Scholasticism on the Continent reached its full flowering in the theology of François Turretini, who was Professor of Theology in Geneva one hundred years after Calvin's death. Turretini chose the theological method of Thomas Aquinas, the medieval Roman Catholic, as the pattern for his own theology. Scripture became a formal principle on which Turretini erected a scientific systematic theology. The authority of Scripture depended not only on its message but also on the claim of a verbal perfection of its literary form. Turretini even claimed inspiration for the vowel signs used in later Hebrew texts, which were not in the original Hebrew manuscripts.

The English Reformation underwent a development quite distinct from that on the Continent. The civil war in the mid-1600s retarded the influence of the new rationalism—and thus slowed the Scholastic reaction to it—until after the period in which the Westminster standards were prepared. English Presbyterian Puritans were open to the embryonic empirical science because it emphasized the practical and experiential, as did Puritanism. But modern science, as we know it, did not develop in England until after the 1660s. The Westminster Divines still belonged to the Reformation era in England. They had more in common with Calvin and the authors of the sixteenth-century confessions than they did with the Post-Reformation Scholastics who soon succeeded them. Until the middle of the seventeenth century in England, the "Age of Faith" prevailed; the "Age of Reason" came quickly but unexpectedly thereafter.

The eighteenth century, during which the American nation was taking form, was the age of science and "Enlightenment." It was a period when human beings felt that they had come to maturity through the use of their reason. Science seemed able to describe and control the world. Knowledge was discovered by experimenting and then by generalizing from data gathered by the five human senses: sight, hearing, touch, taste, and smell.

Philosophically, the attempt to know everything based on sense data alone ended in skepticism. The Scottish philosopher David Hume concluded that all people could know for certain on the basis of sensory experiences alone was that they were having sensory experiences. In reaction to Hume, a Presbyterian minister and professor of philosophy at Glasgow named Thomas Reid developed Scottish Common Sense Philosophy. Reid asserted the exact opposite of Hume. Reid claimed that the senses were completely reliable and that anyone could know the essence of objects exactly as they were. He also believed that all people at all times and in all cultures basically thought alike. This was justified in the name of the "common sense" of humankind.

The preceding discussion would be curious but hardly crucial except for a peculiar historical twist. In 1812, Princeton Theological Seminary was founded as the first ministerial training school of the Presbyterian Church in the U.S.A. Its first and, for a year, its only professor, Archibald Alexander, chose as the twin pillars of its curriculum the systematic theology of François Turretini and the philosophy of Scottish Common Sense. In 1872, Turretini's text was replaced by the three-volume *Systematic Theology* of Charles Hodge, professor for fifty years at Princeton. Hodge was satisfied with Turretini's systematic structure and committed to the method of interpretation provided by "common sense." As a result, Hodge could say confidently:

> The Bible is to the theologian what nature is to the man of science. It is his store-house of facts; and his method of ascertaining what the Bible teaches is the same as that which the natural philosopher adopts to ascertain what nature teaches.

In the mid-nineteenth century the rightness of American "common sense" was challenged by two catastrophic events: the Civil War and Darwin's *Origin of Species.* Most scientists changed from a static commonsense view of the world to a developmental approach which saw reality as constantly changing. Some theologians, including those at Princeton, went on the defensive, clinging to their older methodology. Charles Hodge's son, A. A. Hodge, and his successor, B. B. Warfield, refined a view of the inerrancy of the Bible in the original autographs (the original biblical manuscripts which no longer exist). Their view conflicted violently with the rising discipline of biblical criticism.

Theological differences erupted into an ecclesiastical struggle when Charles A. Briggs of Union Theological Seminary in New York accused Warfield and the Princetonians of teaching a Post-Reformation Scholasticism instead of the theology of Calvin and the Westminster Confession. Historically, Briggs was right, but ecclesiastically he was doomed. Generations of Presbyterian ministers, and through them their elders, had accepted the methods of Turretini and Common Sense as being the style of Calvin and Westminster. Briggs was accused of heresy in the Presbytery of New York. In 1893, after a much-publicized two-year trial, Briggs was convicted of denying the authority of the Bible. In that same year the General Assembly acted to make the Hodge-Warfield theory of the inerrancy of the

Bible normative in the church as the correct interpretation of the Westminster Confession.

For a generation, the Presbyterian Church was severely polarized over the issues of biblical criticism and evolution, which were linked in the popular mind. In 1925, the Scopes trial made the views on evolution of William Jennings Bryan, a Presbyterian elder, seem ludicrous. In that same year a Special Theological Commission was appointed in the Presbyterian Church to deal with the polarization that was threatening the peace and unity of the denomination. In 1927, the commission reported and the Assembly adopted a statement that no one body, not even the General Assembly, had the right to make binding interpretations of the Westminster standards. Only through the judicial process, and in regard to specific issues, could this be done. Theological decision making was decentralized from the Assembly to the presbyteries. The era of theological pluralism was inaugurated in reaction to the bitterness and strife of the previous generation. Many Presbyterians felt that it would be better not to discuss theology at all.

All the foregoing controversy was carried on in the name of the Westminster Confession and Catechisms. Understandably, many in the denomination, even today, are still reacting to the Westminster standards in light of the ecclesiastical struggles of the early twentieth century. Our task is to look again at the work of the Westminster Assembly in its own historical context. There we will discover a confession and catechisms that, although not modern, are majestic in their sense of the sovereignty of God and are useful in their attempt to present a balanced approach to the interpretation of the Bible. Just as we discovered in studying the earlier creeds of the ancient church and the confessions of the sixteenth century, there is much of value here that we can relate to our attempt to live the Christian life today

Historical Context: The Case of the Westminster Confession of Faith and Catechisms

Edward Reynolds sat on a wooden bench on the embankment overlooking the Thames. Behind him rose the Houses of Parliament; if the doors had been open to the fresh spring air, he might have heard the drone of debate. The subject was—and had been for a year—a new confession of faith designed to unify the Church of England under a Presbyterian system of government.

It was March 17, 1648. Reynolds had been one of the Assembly of Divines (ministers of the Church of England), assisted by some Scottish commissioners, who were appointed by Parliament to work on this confession. Alone of all the Assembly members, he had sat on every major committee during its drafting.

Reynolds clenched his fists with impatience. Why, he wondered, after all this time, was the Westminster Confession still marooned in the House of Commons? The Assembly had finished the confession after three years and delivered it to the Houses of Parliament in December 1646. The House of Lords had passed it in February 1647 and asked the Commons to concur. The Scottish commissioners had taken it back to Scotland with them, and on August 27, 1647, it had been adopted by the General Assembly of the Church of Scotland as its confession of faith, supplanting the Scots Confession of 1560.

But still the members of the House of Commons haggled over every paragraph. They seemed to be questioning every Scripture proof, which the Divines had added only at the Commons' insistence—and all the while Oliver Cromwell and his army were breathing at the door, gaining political influence every day and using that influence to purge Presbyterians from Parliament and replace them with Independent Congregationalists. Even now, Reynolds knew, the House of Commons was reduced to a mere hundred members, most of them Cromwell's Independents. He turned to look at the spires of Westminster

Abbey, where the whole project had begun. Did the new confession have a chance to become the doctrinal standard of the Church of England?

The Divine Right of Monarchs: Twilight of an Age

The Elizabethan era (1558–1603) retained the remnants of medieval thought. Elizabethans pictured a Great Chain of Being stretching from the most insignificant inanimate object up to the foot of God's throne. Human beings occupied a niche just below angels on this chain. Monarchs were the highest of humans. Their rights were derived by virtue of their royal birth, as ordained by the law of God. As such, monarchs were responsible not to the governed but to God alone. Active resistance to a king or queen was a sin ensuring damnation.

By the early seventeenth century, however, most English people no longer thought of their ruler as an absolute monarch. The powers of the Crown were limited by the will of God and the laws of nature. They were also circumscribed by the rights of Parliament and the common law, which protected people's property rights. At the same time, Parliament was not superior to the Crown. A "balanced polity" regarded Parliament as a council summoned by the ruler from time to time for the purpose of levying taxes and enacting laws. Under the precedent set by Elizabeth I, Parliament had no right to concern itself with foreign affairs, religion, or other "mysteries of state"; these were the realm of the monarch and her advisers. Even the Parliamentarians—the severest critics of the monarchy—admitted that Parliament could not trespass on the Crown's rights or the rights of the state church.

James VI of Scotland, only son of Mary, Queen of Scots, ascended the throne of England as King James I in 1603. Both king and Parliament were seeking to widen their spheres of power. James was a firm adherent of the doctrine of the divine right of kings. He insisted that his authority came directly from God. According to him, the king was the sole lawgiver, and Parliament was merely a function of ancient custom to be called only if and when the king felt so inclined.

King James was the product of a rigid Calvinist upbringing in Scotland. Now, though, the more fixed he became in his ideas about kingship, the more he detested the teachings of Calvin and the Kirk. But England was changing. The habit of complete obedience to a dynasty had died with Elizabeth I. Order and stability were still important, but the Renaissance and Reformation had awakened a new sense of power in the people. British ships explored the New World. Trade was thriving. A merchant middle class was emerging, eager to manage its own destiny.

Church and State

The Protestant Reformation on the Continent resulted in national Protestant churches. England presented a different pattern. Seeking a divorce from Catherine of Aragon, Henry VIII had come into conflict with the power of the pope. In 1531, when the pope refused to sanction Henry's divorce, Henry declared himself Supreme Head of the Church of England. Thus England had a national church before it had a Reformation. One result was a distinctive form of Protestantism known as Puritanism. Puritans were those who wished to "purify" the Church of England from within by eliminating the remnants of what they saw as Roman Catholic "popery."

When James came to the English throne, the Puritans were initially elated. In 1603, they presented him a Millenary Petition (claiming to represent a thousand ministers) stating Puritan grievances. Elizabeth I had squelched these Puritans, shutting down their printing presses in 1590. Now they were back, demanding a Presbyterian form of church government and a more Reformed theology. They hoped that this new king from Calvinist Scotland would heed their cause.

A milder-tempered king might have listened. But James had had enough of the Kirk, with its alarming notions about the rights of congregations to organize themselves, worship in their own ways, and settle their own church order. He concluded that Calvinism and monarchy would bump heads in the long run. If people could decide for themselves about religion, they might also decide for themselves about politics. James made it clear that the Church of England would remain Episcopal in its government. "No Bishop, no King," became his motto.

The Personal Rule of Charles I

If James I had little use for Parliament, his son Charles had even less. Crowned King Charles I in 1625, he had an annoying way of flaunting his independence in the face of Parliament's increasing power. First, he married the Catholic daughter of Marie de' Medici of France, for reasons of "political alliance." The English people who felt their future peace depended on remaining Protestant watched nervously.

Then Charles latched on to his father's court favorite, George Villiers, the handsome, clever, and extravagant Duke of Buckingham. Villiers's complete failure as a statesman and general made him unpopular with Parliament, yet Charles blindly took his advice. To meet expenses, Villiers suggested that Charles demand forced "loans" from certain subjects. Seventy people who refused him funds were imprisoned. The Parliament of 1628 protested. They forced Charles to sign a Petition of Right admitting that his "arbitrary taxation and imprisonment" violated the "fundamental liberties of the kingdom." Villiers was subsequently assassinated, an act the Puritans agreed was a judgment from God.

The king was frustrated by Parliament. Furious, he resumed levying taxes without their consent. Parliament responded by removing all bishops from their seats in the House of Lords. Charles, remarking that parliaments were "in the nature of cats that ever grow cursed with age," disbanded Parliament altogether and determined to govern without it.

For eleven years, he succeeded. Charles felt that his motives were noble. He meant to exercise his divine right to rule unhampered by Parliamentary harassment. He had no intention of becoming a despot. He enacted generous poor laws, took strict action regarding corruption in high officials, avoided entanglement in foreign wars, and encouraged trade. Prosperity prevailed. But in dispensing with the services of Parliament for eleven years, Charles unbalanced the national polity and provoked both Parliamentarians and Puritans. This proved to be disastrous; Parliament—ever since the early days of Elizabeth—had been the symbol of freedom for Protestant England.

The Puritans and Parliamentary Revolt

One consequence of Charles's personal rule was a lack of money for the government. Without Parliament to levy taxes, he was forced to be extremely frugal. State action was limited to a minimum. The army was reduced to a fragment. Archbishop William Laud formulated a helpful series of "innovations," designed to emphasize Charles's divine right and raise new revenues. Under Queen Elizabeth, everyone was required to attend the Church of England. They could think what they liked, but outwardly they had to conform. By 1625, laxity had set in. Some people did not bother to go to church. Others openly disagreed with its teachings. Laud began to haul before the magistrate all adults caught skipping church, where they were fined one shilling per offense. The Puritans, already dissatisfied, saw Laud's act as open persecution. The Parliamentarians, on the lookout for a way to inflame the nation against the monarchy, began to agitate publicly.

But Archbishop Laud did not stop there. He decided that spiritual conditions in Scotland were too determined by Presbyterianism. In 1637 he announced that the Scots must adopt the Episcopal *Book of Common Prayer.* King Charles, through Laud, only sought liturgical uniformity in his kingdom. He had no interest in doctrinal changes. But the Scots cried "Popery!" When the prayer book was first read at St. Giles's Catheral in Edinburgh, a riot broke out. Scots flocked to subscribe to a National Covenant in defense of the "true Reformed religion." Charles ordered the Scottish Assembly to disband. It refused. The king would not condone rebellion and called in his troops. The Scots, although still loyal to the king, met the English army with banners proclaiming "For Christ's Crown and Covenant." Two skirmishes followed (the First and Second Bishops' Wars), in which the Scots completely routed the English army. Among the humiliating terms of the Treaty of Ripon was a clause that the king must again call a Parliament.

Charles had to comply because he had promised to pay the victorious Scots—still camped on English soil—a huge sum of money, and only a vote of Parliament could release the funds. The "Long Parliament," as it came to be known, convened in 1640. Its members arrived with large lists of grievances accumulated over their eleven-year absence. The tempers of the majority in the House were Puritan and Presbyterian. They were critical of the king's policies, his ministers, and the incompetencies that had caused the two Scottish wars. An Act of Attainder was passed against the Earl of Strafford; the king was forced to allow his loyal minister to be executed without a trial. Other royal ministers quickly left the country. The king, hoping a policy of concession and moderation might regain Parliament's trust, began to give way.

But in October of 1641, Parliament presented Charles

with a document called the Grand Remonstrance. This long list of grievances included a petition demanding the calling of a synod to implement a purification of the Church of England. The Remonstrance passed by a mere eleven votes. It split the House and solidified conflicting political camps. Royalist Episcopalians were set against Parliamentarian Presbyterians. And the radical Independent Congregationalists surfaced as a third potential political force.

For some members of Parliament, the Grand Remonstrance was not enough. Oliver Cromwell and his Independents were unwilling to let the matter rest. The king still had not yielded to their full demands for the reform of the church. They wanted each individual and each local congregation to be free to worship according to conscience. They regarded the bishops as tyrants and feared the real designs of the royal court and its "popish" entourage. Then the Scottish commissioners convinced Parliament that every member must sign a Solemn League and Covenant which would bind England and Scotland to secure a uniform confession of faith, a form of church government, and a directory for worship and catechizing. Cromwell strongly objected. The Covenant implied a Presbyterian government with no allowance for individual worship according to one's conscience. Religious toleration, which the Independents prized above all else, was to be sacrificed to national unity. Cromwell concluded that nothing short of a military victory over the king could secure a free Christian community.

Opposing Cromwell and his Independents were the Royalists. They were content with the Episcopal government of the Church of England, and they were loyal to their monarch—right or wrong. For them, the issue was the divine right of monarchs to rule and the legitimacy of the Episcopal form of church government. They were prepared to fight for their beliefs.

In the middle stood the Presbyterian Puritans. They felt that Charles had been punished enough for his eleven years of "tyranny." The time had come for king and Parliament to work together to reform the church and the country. This group dominated the Parliament. They decided to call an assembly to convene at Westminster Abbey in London for the purpose of formulating a plan for the reformation of the Church of England to make it more Presbyterian in government and more reformed in its theology. Between June 1642 and May 1643 the Parliament passed five different bills calling for the convening of this Assembly of Divines. Each time, King Charles refused to sign the bill. Finally, a sixth bill was prepared and passed as an ordinance of the House of Commons. When it was agreed to by the House of Lords on June 12, 1643, it was put into effect without the king's assent.

A Civil War and a Confession of Faith

The Westminster Assembly first met in July 1643. The members gathered in Henry VII's Chapel in Westminster Abbey. Later, with the advent of cold weather, the Assembly transferred its place of meeting to the more comfortable Jerusalem Chamber in the adjoining Deanery of Westminster, where it continued to sit for the remainder of its existence. The Assembly was composed of 121 Puritan ministers of the Church of England, most of whom were Presbyterian in their sentiments, but with some Congregationalists and a few favoring Episcopal church government. In addition there were 30 lay members of Parliament, including three Erastians. (These men were so-called because they espoused the belief, attributed to the Swiss physician Thomas Erastus and held by many in Parliament, that the final authority in ecclesiastical matters rested with the civil authorities.) In addition there were six Scottish advisers. In calling the Assembly, Parliament envisioned a national church, embracing all people, with a simple liturgy, presbyteries rather than bishops, and a Reformed creed. Their vision did not include toleration of religious groups other than those represented in the Assembly. Too much religious toleration opened the door to trouble-causing sects and radical reformers like the Anabaptists and Quakers. The Roman Catholic Church, they believed, would be only too willing to use any instance of religious anarchy as a wedge to split the Church of England. The task, then, was one of maintaining order in a potentially chaotic situation.

The Westminster Assembly was merely an advisory arm to Parliament and was directly responsible to that body. Parliament selected its members, appointed its officers, proposed its topics for discussion, and delineated the scope of its work.

The first task given the Assembly by Parliament was to revise the Thirty-nine Articles, the creed of the Church of England. The Divines had reached Article XVI when the political situation changed. Parliament was now fully engaged in a civil war with Charles I, and its military fortunes were at a low ebb. It needed the aid of Scotland. The price which the Scots put on that aid was the Solemn League and Covenant. Scottish commissioners who were dispatched to London as representatives to the English Parliament also served on a Grand Committee which coordinated the work of the Assembly with that of Parliament. Eventually some of the commissioners sat in the Westminster Assembly as guests with the right to debate, though they did not vote. Four Scottish commissioners were Presbyterian ministers and actively served on the committee to draft a Confession of Faith.

Doctrinally, the Assembly was amazingly unified. Its battles were fought over matters of polity. One "Grand Debate," thirty days in length, ensued over whether Presbyterian polity was sanctioned by divine right. Many hours were spent in prayer, worship, and fasting. Assembly member Robert Baillie recorded one worship service eight hours long, without a single break. Sermons of one hour and prayers two hours in length were the rule. Of the sixty members in average daily attendance, eleven men did the bulk of the actual writing of the confession of faith. Seven were English, four were clerical Scottish commissioners. When the Assembly finished its drafting in 1647, it had produced for Parliament the Westminster Confession of Faith as its guide in doctrine, a Shorter Catechism for teaching youth, a Larger Catechism as an aid for preaching, a Directory for Public Worship, a form for Presbyterian church government, and a Psalter to provide biblical psalms to be sung in public worship.

The Westminster Confession of Faith was composed in thirty-three chapters. It began with Chapter I on Scripture, which was the source from which all other truths were derived. A second section, Chapters II through V, declared the sovereignty of God. It spoke of God's decrees, or plans, or purposes, displayed in the creation of the world and in providential care of God's people. A central section, Chapters VI through XX, addressed the working out of God's purposes in human history. Chapters VI and VII described the fall of humanity into sin and God's covenant to redeem them. In Chapter VIII, Jesus Christ the mediator of God's covenant was presented as the pinnacle of God's purposeful work on behalf of humanity. Then Chapters XI through XX described the way of salvation in Christ and how it became effective in the lives of believers. A fourth section of the confession, Chapters XXI through XXVI, dealt with ethical dimensions of the Christian life. It treated topics such as the Law of God, liberty of conscience, church and state, and marriage and divorce. The final section, Chapters XXVII through XXXV, treated the church, the sacraments, and last things. The confession provided a concise system of theology. Yet the concern of the Divines that theology be a practical rather than theoretical science was manifested by the fact that nearly two thirds of the confession dealt with practical matters of the Christian life in its personal and social dimensions.

The Divines produced a Larger Catechism which was even longer than the Confession of Faith. This catechism was to provide guidance for preachers in expounding on the doctrines stated in the confession. The Assembly gave more time to this document than to the confession. Questions 1–5 expounded what the Scriptures principally teach; Questions 6–90 responded with what Christians are to believe; Questions 91–196 dealt with the practical duties of living the Christian life.

The last of the Scottish commissioners left the Assembly in November 1647. The Shorter Catechism was not yet finished. It was understood to be a simple summary statement for young people of what was contained in the Larger Catechism. The actual work of compiling it was left largely to one person. The Assembly spent very little time on it, because all questions of substance had already been debated at length. Its structure paralleled that of the Larger Catechism. Questions 1–38 dealt with what Christians were to believe, while Questions 39–107 concerned the duties of the Christian life.

On March 17, 1648, when Edward Reynolds sat uneasily on his bench outside the chambers of Parliament, members of the Assembly elsewhere in the city were still wrestling with the Scripture proofs which the House of Commons required them to affix to the catechisms, as they had done with the Confession of Faith. Others could handle that task, Reynolds thought. He was much more concerned with how the Commons would finally vote on the confession.

Reynolds's mind whirled with questions. What would happen? Cromwell and his New Model Army, once the servants of Parliament, had organized as an independent political power. They had seized King Charles. Rumors were circulating that they wanted his head. "Liberty of conscience! Religious toleration!" they shouted. Edwards could not face the potential anarchy he believed might come with such toleration. England had always had an established church. He and the Presbyterians only wanted that establishment to be reformed according to Scripture by introducing a government by presbyteries. Cromwell did not really oppose that. It was just that Cromwell also wanted toleration for all to believe and worship as they pleased.

Reynolds sighed. Perhaps it would have been better to have come to a compromise with Cromwell and his powerful army. It was apparently too late for that now. The Presbyterians were divided among themselves about what to do. Some wanted to help restore the monarch. Others would make an arrangement with Cromwell. Still others believed that they could yet enforce a uniform Presbyterian settlement on the English church. But most of their influential friends were no longer in Parliament. It was populated with a majority of Independents.

The monarch in chains, the church in turmoil, the country at war with itself . . . where would it end? And what of the confession? In the face of such chaos, could it have any impact? Or was the Westminster Assembly just a lame duck, and was its confession obsolete even as it was completed?

Edward Reynolds's worst fears were realized. At first all went well. On June 20, 1648, the House of Commons accepted the Confession of Faith to which the Lords had already assented. The political situation, however, worsened. In December, Cromwell's army essentially took over the House of Commons. Then, in 1649, King Charles was beheaded. Presbyterians who had hoped to remain loyal both to the king and to their Puritan convictions were devastated. The work of the Assembly had been accepted, but there was no political force left in the Parliament to cause it to be implemented. For five and a half years the Assembly had met on the average of four times a week. Now, it was difficult to get a quorum. Some members continued to meet on Thursday mornings as a committee to examine candidates for the ministry. On March 25, 1652, the Assembly informally broke up. One month later Cromwell dissolved Parliament and took power as Lord Protector from 1653 until his death in 1658. During this period, Presbyterians who refused to support Cromwell's Commonwealth were ejected from their parishes.

Near the end of Cromwell's life, he gave reluctant consent to a petition to issue a confession of faith for the whole kingdom. The result was the Savoy Declaration, prepared by a committee composed primarily of Independent former members of the Westminster Assembly. It was simply the Westminster Confession of Faith with changes to make it conform to Congregational church government.

Cromwell died in September 1658. His son Richard reigned for less than eight months. Then England was plunged into anarchy. The Long Parliament was finally restored on February 21, 1660. The Westminster Confession of Faith was again adopted and ordered printed. On March 14, 1660, Presbyterian church government was established by law. Two days later the Parliament dissolved itself. The restoration of the monarchy was clearly coming, and a lasting church settlement would have to wait until the Restoration was accomplished.

Parliament convened on April 25, 1660, and declared itself for government by King, Lords, and Commons. Presbyterians supported the Restoration and hoped for a "Comprehension." That would mean a limited Episcopacy with bishops as presidents of synods composed of presbyters. Presbyterians and Episcopalians could join in this, with Independents excluded, though perhaps tolerated outside the national church.

On May 29, 1660, King Charles's son, Charles II, who had been in exile in France, returned to London in triumph. Within a few weeks, ten Presbyterian divines had been included among the King's Chaplains. As soon as an Episcopal church was reestablished, however, the Presbyterians' hopes were dashed. The vengeful bishops saw to it that on May 19, 1662, an Act of Uniformity was passed demanding complete conformity to a pre-1640s version of Episcopacy, with all the ecclesiastical and theological aspects to which the Puritans had objected. On St. Bartholomew's Day, Sunday, August 24, 1662, about two thousand ministers, over one fifth of the clergy of the Church of England, were ejected from their parishes for nonconformity. They were impoverished and disgraced and in the end could only make common cause with the Independents, Baptists, and other nonconformists whom earlier they had opposed. Some of the members of the Westminster Assembly conformed to the newly established church. Among them was Edward Reynolds, who eventually became a bishop in the Church of England.

Essential Tenets of the Reformed Faith

The Sovereignty of God

The Westminster Divines had a philosophy of history. God was in charge. They reflected their confidence in God's sovereign power and care in all they said and did. They thought and wrote in a prescientific world. They did not attempt to present an accurate description of natural causation; rather, they sought to affirm, with the biblical writers and other Reformed theologians, that all was in God's hands. In that they trusted.

Certainly the language and thought forms that the Westminster Divines used were those of their own century. Calvin, for example, had used the term "decree" infrequently. But in the seventeenth century, decrees were the standard terms by which theologians referred to God's activity. Such terms may sound mechanical or harsh to us now. It is useful, therefore, for us to note how careful the Divines were to avoid the extreme theological positions that were common in the seventeenth century. The Westminster Confession is much less rigid on issues regarding

God's sovereignty, for example, than the canons of Dort, formulated at the Synod of Dort, or Dordrecht, in the Netherlands in 1618–19. Several examples may illustrate the moderation of the Westminster Confession of Faith.

Some have assumed that the Westminster Confession of Faith takes the position of "supralapsarianism." The word "lapse" refers to the fall of humankind into sin. The issue is, When did God decide to elect a company of people to salvation? The "supra" position is the necessary position to hold if one argues deductively from a doctrine of the sovereignty of God. If God knows everything and is in charge of everything, then God knew who would be saved and decreed their election even before he created the world. Some members of the Westminster Assembly, including their Moderator, William Twisse, held such a position. But the majority did not. The Confession of Faith reflects the deductive thinking of that age, but it also argues inductively from Scripture that God created the world, people fell into sin, and then God decided, or decreed, to send Christ for their salvation. That position is called "infralapsarianism." It understands God to be One who responds in mercy and grace to the inexplicable act of human sin.

Another distinctive of a "hyper" or excessively rigid Calvinism is the doctrine of the double decree. Again, the issue is whether the logical implications of a concept must be drawn out or whether one can live with the biblical witness and allow some human curiosity to go unsatisfied. Logic dictates that if God is Sovereign, and if God has decreed that some are elected to salvation, it must be that God has decreed that others are elected to damnation. The difficulty with this position is that Scripture never states that God chooses some to damnation. The Westminster Confession draws deductions from the concept of decrees which most of us would not. However, in moderation by seventeenth-century standards, the confession also says that God passes by those who are unsaved.

The Westminster Confession of Faith avoids attributing an arbitrary determinism to God as a corollary of God's sovereignty. The confession states that the rule of God in the universe is such that no "violence is offered to the will of the creature, nor is the liberty or contingency of second causes taken away, but rather established." People have free will, according to the Westminster Confession. When speaking of God's providence, the confession states not only that secondary causes have their own validity but that circumstances may happen "either necessarily, freely, or contingently."

The sovereignty of God in the Westminster Confession of Faith is a doctrine of comforting confidence, not one of dictatorial determinism. We would certainly not express our faith in God's providential care in just the same way that the Westminster Divines did in the mid-seventeenth century. When we understand the moderation of their meaning, however, we can find in them a model of attempting to be faithful to the full teaching of Scripture without adding to it human logical implications which distort the comfort of the Christian gospel.

The Authority and Interpretation of Scripture

In their doctrine of Scripture, the Westminster Divines placed primary emphasis on two motifs or themes: the first five sections of the confession are an ascending development on the theme of the Holy Spirit's relationship to Scripture; the last five sections deal with the interpretation of Scripture in light of its purpose of bringing us to salvation in Christ. It may be useful to review briefly the substance of the ten subsections of Chapter I of the Westminster Confession of Faith, "Of the Holy Scripture."

The favorite theologian of the Divines was Augustine, closely followed by Calvin. The Westminster theologians followed Augustine and Calvin in Section 1 on the "light of nature." That phrase refers to a direct revelation of God in the human heart. This sense of the divine is suppressed by human sin but can never be wholly eradicated. The "works of creation and providence" only reinforce in people what they already know in their hearts. God's Word is like a pair of spectacles, or contact lenses, which focus, reinforce, and make clear what was previously only dimly perceived. For the Westminster Divines, there were not two sources of revelation, nature and Scripture, but only one: God's Word. God's Word is implanted in the human heart and reinforced by the Word of God in Scripture. Christ and Scripture were both known as the Word of God for the Divines. As Edward Reynolds declared, "Preaching of the Word is called preaching of Christ."

In Section 2, the Westminster Divines did not speculate on how we got the canon, the sixty-six books in our present Bible. They simply followed Calvin and the Reformed confessions in asserting that Scripture was given by inspiration of God and did not depend for its authority on the authority of the church. Inspiration was not defined as to its mode but only affirmed in its result. It was the Word of God for faith and life.

Section 3 excluded the Apocrypha from the canon, because the Divines did not consider these books divinely inspired. The confession followed the open attitude of Calvin, which affirmed the inspiration of Scripture's divine message but left theologians free to deal with critical questions through scholarship.

Section 4 affirmed that the authority of Scripture was not dependent on the testimony of any person or church but on God, the author of Scripture. That was another way of saying that we do not have to prove the Bible is true by recourse to logical reasons or external evidences of the Bible's authority. It is enough that when we read it we encounter God, whom Reynolds called the "Narrator" of Scripture.

Section 5 climaxed the development of the first half of the Westminster Confession's statement on Scripture.

While many arguments for the truth of Scripture may be produced, only the witness of the Holy Spirit in the human heart can finally persuade a person that Scripture is the Word of God. The Westminster Divines stood with Calvin in stating that "our full persuasion and assurance" of the authority of Scripture comes from the internal testimony of the Holy Spirit. Samuel Rutherford, one of the Scottish commissioners, in a tract against the Roman Catholics, answered the question, "How do we know that Scripture is the Word of God?" If ever there was a place where one might expect to find Scholastic arguments in the medieval Roman Catholic style, it would be here. Instead, Rutherford simply appealed to the Spirit of Christ speaking through Scripture to the human subject: "Sheep are docile creatures, Ioh.10.27. *My sheep heare my voyce, I know them and they follow me* . . . , so the instinct of Grace knoweth the voyce of the Beloved amongst many voyces, *Cant.* 2.8, and this discerning power is *in the Subject.*"

Section 6 begins the discussion of how Scripture may be interpreted in light of its purpose to bring people to salvation and guide them in living the Christian life. The content of Scripture is clearly delineated: "The whole counsel of God, concerning all things necessary for his own glory, man's salvation, faith, and life." Scripture was not an encyclopedia of answers to every sort of question for the Divines. Some things had to be ordered by reason and Christian prudence. Samuel Rutherford, for example, was very explicit that Scripture's purpose was to mediate salvation, not communicate information on science. He listed areas in which Scripture is *not* our rule: for example, "not in things of Art and Science, as to speak Latine, to demonstrate conclusions of Astronomie." But Scripture is our rule, according to Rutherford, "1. in fundamentalls of salvation. 2. In all morals of both first and second table."

In Sections 7 and 8, the Divines acknowledged that there were two levels on which the Bible could be approached. First was the central saving message of the gospel. That was available to anyone, "not only the learned, but the unlearned" who desired to know it, through the "due use of ordinary means." That latter phrase in the mid-seventeenth century meant going to church and listening to a sermon which explained the Christian message. But there were also parts of the Bible which were not plain. For the Divines, those related not to the central message of Christ but to the surrounding historical and cultural context. These were the matters that caused "controversies in religion." In such controversies the Divines recommended recourse to scholarship. Study the Bible in Greek and Hebrew. Many of the Divines were extraordinarily learned for their time in the languages and cultural background of the biblical period and were well aware of the impact of such influences on the biblical writers. Sermons of the Divines illustrate their commitment to follow wherever careful scholarly study of the biblical text led them, even if it raised theological problems. Sections 7 and 8 exemplified the constant dual concern of the Divines: to meet the demands of careful scholarship where that was appropriate and to meet the spiritual needs of ordinary people.

In Section 9, the Westminster Confession contended that Scripture is a unity. Particular texts have a single, not multiple, meaning, and the meaning of particular texts should be sought in the light of the general meaning of Scripture as a whole. That is a reflection of the general Reformation principle called the "analogy of faith." The wording of this section of the Westminster Confession bears strong similarities to Chapter II of the Second Helvetic Confession and Chapter XVII of the Scots Confession of 1560. For the Westminster Divines, the Bible was a book that told one unified story: the saving grace and mercy of God in Jesus Christ. They referred to that theme sometimes as the gospel and sometimes as the covenant. But verses of Scripture were not to be taken individually as proof texts for a preconceived theology. "The infallible rule of interpretation of Scripture is the Scripture itself" meant that people must always look to the whole of the biblical message.

In the final section on Scripture, 10, the Divines end where they began with an affirmation of the union of the Spirit and the Word. They concluded, "The Supreme Judge, by which all controversies of religion are to be determined . . . can be no other but the Holy Spirit speaking in the Scripture." The balance of Word and Spirit which the Westminster Divines displayed is the more remarkable because of the pressures exerted on them from opponents on both sides. On the one side were the Roman Catholics and High Church Anglicans who gave an independent role in religion to reason and the pronouncements of the church. On the other side were sectarians, like the seventeenth-century Quakers, who gave an independent role in religion to the Spirit as an inner light within them. For the Westminster Divines, the final judge in controversies of religion was neither the bare word of Scripture interpreted by human logic nor the Spirit speaking apart from the Word. The final judge was the living Word of God, the Spirit of Christ leading persons through the central witness of Scripture to himself.

Contemporary Relevance

To Glorify God

Many have contended that the central theme of Reformed theology is the sovereignty of God. To modern people that often has an uncongenial ring. The word "sovereignty" comes from a seventeenth-century context of royalty and divine right which to Americans carries a connotation of arbitrariness and injustice, but the meaning is far different. The Westminster Divines were protesting arbitrariness and injustice in their world. They certainly did not attribute those same undesirable qualities to God.

The meaning of the sovereignty of God is, at root, that all human beings are, at every moment of our lives, in relationship to the living God. The image of God in humanity is not some particular quality or attribute such as reason, free will, or the ability to dominate nature. Jesus Christ *is* the image of God according to Scripture (2 Cor. 4:4; Col. 1:15). It was not that he was smarter, freer, or more dominant than other people. What distinguished Jesus from his contemporaries was that he was totally obedient to God who had sent him. The image of God, and the meaning of our humanity, is that we are created in relationship to God. When we obey God, as Jesus did, we "image" God in our lives.

The thrust of Reformed theology is that we glorify God by living lives of obedient activity. That has not always been the Christian viewpoint. Thomas Aquinas, the greatest representative of medieval Scholasticism, announced that "man's ultimate felicity consists only in the contemplation of God." To think about God, to meditate on God, to enjoy God in the privacy of prayer have been, for many, the supreme purpose of religion. Not so for Calvin and Reformed theology. Obedient activity has priority over contemplation. The well-known words of the first answer of the Westminster Shorter Catechism put the two emphases in their proper Reformed order: "Man's chief end is to glorify God, and to enjoy him forever." We glorify God by living in obedience to God's will, and enjoyment of God comes as a by-product.

Every seminary student has heard the story of the candidate for the ministry in early America being asked by an older presbyter if the candidate would be willing to be "damned for the glory of God." Students rejoice in the thought that the candidate might have replied that he would be willing that the whole presbytery should be damned to the glory of God! We are well aware that God takes no pleasure and receives no glory by being estranged from a single person. But what those early Calvinists were striving to emphasize has a valid point. We ought not to be self-centeredly interested only in our own personal salvation. We are saved to serve. We should be seeking the glory of God by working toward the kingdom of God. God cares for us and will meet our needs. We need to show our gratitude by acting on God's agenda for this world. That is the meaning of the Reformed doctrine of the sovereignty of God.

To Interpret the Bible

In 1978, both denominations coming together to form the Presbyterian Church (U.S.A.) initiated studies of the interpretation of Scripture. The study done under the auspices of the Advisory Council of Discipleship and Worship of the former United Presbyterian Church in the U.S.A. was received by the General Assembly in 1982 and its guidelines adopted. The report, *Biblical Authority and Interpretation,* is available as a resource document from the Advisory Council on Discipleship and Worship in New York. A parallel activity carried on through the Council on Theology and Culture of the former Presbyterian Church in the U.S. was reported to the reuniting General Assembly in 1983. It wisely did not rework ground already covered in the previous year's report but, rather, greatly expanded and elaborated the very brief guidelines for interpreting Scripture already adopted. The report, *Presbyterian Understanding and Use of Holy Scripture* was sent to every congregation and is available from the Office of the General Assembly in Atlanta.

The earlier report offered a short list of seven principles of interpretation derived from the Reformed confessions in our *Book of Confessions.* Since the primary concern of this present study is to find elements of practical value and utility in those confessions, let us look at those seven principles which remain of importance to us. The later study should be used further to develop our understanding of these and other principles of sound biblical interpretation.

All seven of these basic rules of biblical interpretation

are meant to be taken together. One, taken in isolation from the others, could be used to produce a distorted and potentially divisive method of biblical interpretation. The desire of the church, reflected in its confessions, is to develop a balanced and wholesome approach which does justice to all that Scripture is and can be for us.

1. Recognize that Jesus Christ, the Redeemer, is the center of Scripture (Scots 3.18; Barmen 8.05; C '67 9.27). The Bible is not about everything. It is about Jesus Christ. It tells us the story of salvation and the life of faith. It guides us in being rightly related to God and to our neighbor. Scripture has a center and it has surrounding material. All parts of the Bible are to be understood in relation to the central theme that binds it together: God's good creation, human sin, and God's redemptive activity in Jesus Christ.

2. Let the focus be on the plain text of Scripture (Scots 3.18; WCF 6.007, 6.009). We must always begin with the text in its grammatical and historical context. The first principle, that Christ is the center, rules out a surface literalism which treats every word of the Bible as equal to every other word. This second principle rules out allegorism, subjectivism, and personal flights of fancy. In the early church and the Middle Ages, theologians often succumbed to the temptation of using allegory. It is a method of interpretation that views an object, a person, or an event in the Old Testament as really representing an object, person, event, or principle in the present, with little or no attempt made to show any actual relationship between the two. A familiar example is the use of the love poem in the Song of Songs to speak not of the passion of a man and woman for each other but rather, symbolically, of the love of Christ for the church. We remain in danger of avoiding issues in Scripture we do not want to face, or papering over awkward difficulties we discover, and of riding our own private hobbyhorses instead of reporting what the Bible, in

its totality, actually says. The Reformed confessions remind us to take seriously the plain text of Scripture.

3. Depend on the guidance of the Holy Spirit in interpreting and applying God's message (Scots 3.18; WCF 6.005, 6.010; C '67 9.30). Reformed theology acknowledges that we accept the authority of Scripture because of the inward testimony or persuasion of the Holy Spirit. That is a theological way of saying what we observe behaviorally. If a person or book meets our needs, that person or book has authority for us. This principle from the confessions says that the same Holy Spirit will open our minds to understand and put our hearts in a mood to receive the truth of God in Scripture. The Spirit does not come to enable us to skip our homework or avoid the hard work of serious Bible study. But the Spirit will enable us to approach that study with an open attitude and an enabling motivation.

4. Be guided by the doctrinal consensus of the church, which is the "rule of faith" (Scots 3.18; HC 4.022). We are not the first persons ever to think about these things; we have a body of wisdom on which to draw. The Heidelberg Catechism evidences a wholesome attitude in answering its Question 22: "What, then, must a Christian believe?" The answer is: "All that is promised us in the gospel, a summary of which is taught us in the articles of the Apostles' Creed, our universally acknowledged confession of faith." The theological tradition of the church, embodied in its creeds and confessions, shows a remarkable consensus on what the main teachings of Scripture are. That same confessional tradition, when viewed as a whole, will help us to recognize and avoid many of the tangential and potentially troublesome side streams of doctrine on which Christians have never attained consensus. We can be helped by observing the "rule of faith."

5. Let all interpretations be in accord with the "rule of love," the twofold commandment to love God and to love

our neighbor (Scots 3.18; 2d Helv. 5.010). Augustine, whose thought summed up the theology of the early church and guided much of the early Middle Ages, articulated the rule of love. In contemporary language, his concern was something like this: If you hear someone interpreting Scripture in a way that does not elevate love for God or enhance love for neighbor, you should question the validity of that interpretation. It is no good to say that even though a person may behave in a hateful and harmful way, the theology of that person is sound. Nonsense! "You will know them by their fruits" is still a biblical principle (Matt. 7:20). Suppose someone says, "Why, some of my best friends are blacks [or women, or Jews, etc.], but it's just that the Bible puts them in an inferior place in the scheme of things." The rule of love would say, "Look out, something strange is going on here." Again, we must take all seven principles of biblical interpretation together. If we used only the rule of love, no doubt we would soon discover that different people had different notions of what love would allow. But taken with all the other principles, the rule of love provides a necessary caution, reminding us to look at the results, not just the theory, when evaluating the correctness of someone's interpretation.

6. Remember that interpretation of the Bible requires earnest study (2d Helv. 5.010; WCF 6.008; C '67 9.29). The Protestant Reformers had been trained in the attitude and techniques of Renaissance humanism. They assumed that the correct interpretation of the whole Bible required the most rigorous application of human scholarship. The confessions assume that we must use the tools of scholarship to establish the best text and to interpret the influence of the historical and cultural context in which the divine message has come. The Westminster Confession reminds us that there are two levels at which the Bible functions. The central saving message, "those things which are necessary to be known, believed, and observed, for salvation," are clear to ordinary people who want to know, as well as to

scholars. But in "controversies of religion," in those things which are not "plain in themselves, nor alike clear unto all," we must resort to those in the Christian community who by temperament and training are meticulous students of the mysteries of other languages and cultures to help us.

7. Seek to interpret a particular passage of the Bible in light of all the Bible (Scots 3.18; 2d Helv. 5.010; WCF 6.009; C '67 9.28, 9.29). This principle was added by the standing committee of the General Assembly which processed this report in 1982. It was that committee's way of underlining the theme which runs throughout this report. Take the Bible as a whole and apply the principles of interpretation as a package, not using some in isolation from the others. This principle of comparing Scripture with Scripture is sometimes called the "analogy of faith." It assumes what the first of these seven principles announces, that there is a center to Scripture which gives us perspective on the parts. The direction provided by these seven principles of biblical interpretation can be summed up by a passage from Bullinger's sixteenth-century Reformed perspective in the Second Helvetic Confession:

> But we hold that interpretation of the Scripture to be orthodox and genuine which is gleaned from the Scriptures themselves (from the nature of the language in which they were written, likewise according to the circumstances in which they were set down, and expounded in the light of like and unlike passages and of many and clearer passages) and which agree with the rule of faith and love, and contributes much to the glory of God and man's salvation. (Chapter II)

III

Contemporary Declarations

9

The Theological Declaration of Barmen *A.D. 1934*

May 1984 marked the fiftieth anniversary of The Theological Declaration of Barmen. On May 29–31, 1934, representatives from eighteen German provincial churches—Lutheran, Reformed, and United (Lutheran and Reformed)—met in the industrial city of Barmen-Wuppertal as the First Confessing Synod of the German Evangelical Church. They were protesting interference in the life of the churches by the Nazi government and the errors of the Nazi-inspired "German Christian" movement. They clarified their faith on the basis of the ancient and Reformation confessions and reconfessed it in a new declaration of faith in the face of the concrete errors of the time.

The declaration, more precisely translated, was a "clarification," or "explanation" (*Erklärung* in German), of the meaning of the older confessions as applied to a concrete evil that threatened Christians in 1934. The action of the delegates at Barmen proved to be so right in their time, and so useful as a warning for Christians at all times, that we have included their declaration in our *Book of Confessions*. Their style of clarifying faith in the face of current problems in church and society served as a model to American Presbyterians in the writing of the Confession of 1967.

Celebration of the Barmen Synod's resistance to political tyranny and theological error took place at the 196th General Assembly of the Presbyterian Church (U.S.A.) in 1984, when the Reverend Leopold Esselbach, an ecumenical delegate from the Evangelical Church of Germany, addressed the Assembly. He honored the clergy and laity who gathered in Barmen fifty years before. "They confessed Jesus Christ as Lord of the whole world and of their lives," he said. "Most members of the church still thought it possible to combine their Christian faith with German nationalism. We are mindful that our Protestant churches share in the guilt of those times, and we must humble ourselves before the judgment of God." Esselbach concluded, "Today the Barmen Declaration confronts us with the question: What are the heresies and temptations of our world, so that we may not fall into them?"

Historical Context: The Case of the Barmen Declaration

On May 29, 1934, 139 evangelical clergy and laity met in Barmen-Wuppertal in northern Germany. Because of the growing strength of Adolf Hitler's government and its increasing hostility to the church, the Christians gathered at Barmen felt compelled to issue a clarifying confession of faith. Their purpose was to confront issues then plaguing what they constituted as the First Confessing Synod of the German Evangelical Church: Who is Lord—God or the state? What is the relation of the church to the state? Who or what constitutes revelation?

The Rise of National Socialism

Late to emerge as a nation-state, Germany compensated with a most fervent brand of nationalism and racial pride. United first under the autocratic Hohenzollerns of Prussia, the Germans perpetuated the antidemocratic views of Metternich and developed a centralized political government under the Kaisers and their theory of divine right. Seeking a place in the sun, Germany found itself thrown into the entangling alliances that eventually ushered it to defeat in World War I. The unfavorable armistice terms created a wave of resentment in Germany, not only against the treaty and its signers but also against the Weimar Republic. Defending their national pride, many Germans supported the notion of defeat from within, believing they were sold out by government leaders and a faction of international Jewry.

One of the products of this historic conflict was a young Austrian named Adolf Hitler. Moody and ambitious, yet lethargic and insecure, Hitler grew up feeling persecuted and scorned by much of society. He founded the National Socialist Party in 1919, dedicated to race, blood, and soil. Hitler felt he had a mission to regenerate the German people and save them from Marxists, Jews, Capitalists, Democrats, and Freemasons. Hitler's hatred of the Jews was central. In *Mein Kampf* (My Struggle), published in 1925, he wrote, "The Jew today is the great agitator for the complete destruction of Germany. It was the Jews who plotted the First World War, and they are the power behind Germany's two arch-enemies: international capitalism and international Bolshevism."

Hitler believed that Germany would become a great power only when it had been welded into a powerful military nation. The necessary initial steps were to be purification of the race, elimination of class distinctions, removal of divisive elements such as political parties and religious denominations, and a new system of education. After internal reform was accomplished, Germany was to embark on a program of territorial expansion by means of war. Hitler declared, "All life may be summed up in three propositions: conflict is the father of all things, virtue is a matter of blood, and leadership is primary and decisive."

The "German Christians"

The defeat of Germany in 1918 had been a severe blow to the state church, which had blended Christianity with nationalism. The constitution of the German Reich on August 11, 1919, brought an end to the state church. Some denominations, such as Roman Catholic, Lutheran, and Reformed, were still supported by civil tax monies, while "free churches" such as Methodist and Baptist were not. A German Evangelical Federation of Churches was formed at Wittenberg in 1922. It did not restrict the independence of the twenty-eight regional Protestant churches *(Landeskirchen)* but was intended to enable them to act in concert on matters of common interest.

Parallel to the rise of National Socialism politically was the rise of the so-called "German Christians" in the churches. The "Faith Movement" of these people was born June 6, 1932, with the publication of guiding principles for the movement. The principles reflected the main points of National Socialist Party propaganda: anti-Marx, anti-Jew, anti-internationalism, anti-Freemasonry; for racial purity and "positive Christianity." The "German Christians," created at the initiative of the National Socialist Party, amalgamated various groups which were nationalistic in tendency.

At this time there were few who saw in a Nazi victory a threat to the church. Most church people, while critical of National Socialism, recognized values in it and viewed it as offering great opportunities for the church in the future.

In 1932, a publisher and Christian layman, Leopold Klotz, sought a platform for debate with National Socialism. He published a two-volume work entitled *The Church and the Third Reich: Questions and Demands of German Theologians.* One of the contributors was Paul Tillich, who formulated ten theses to express his opposition to Hitler. Describing the situation as a struggle between socialism and Nazism, Tillich felt that a Protestantism which opened its arms to the latter and rejected the former was betraying its commission to the world. This stance "must lead to the future dissolution of German Protestantism," Tillich warned. "To the extent to which it justifies nationalism and an ideology of blood and race by a doctrine of divine orders of creation, it surrenders its prophetic basis in favor of a new manifest or veiled paganism and betrays its commission to be a witness for the *one* God and the *one* mankind."

Between the Times

Theological as well as political movements affected the churches in the period between 1917 and 1933. Karl Barth published the first edition of his *Commentary on the Epistle to the Romans* in 1919. This work pointed new directions for European Protestant theology. In the fall of 1922, Barth, Friedrich Gogarten, and Eduard Thurneysen founded a periodical, *Zwischen den Zeiten* (Between the Times). This journal became a voice for the developing "dialectical theology," which opposed the traditional beliefs of German liberal Protestantism.

A renaissance of interest in the sixteenth-century Protestant Reformers affected theological developments. The Berlin church historian Karl Holl (1896–1926) published a series of essays on Luther which challenged the liberal interpretation of the reformer and questioned the individualism of the day. New editions of Luther's works appeared. There was a parallel rediscovery of Calvin. New editions of Calvin's works were published and edited by Wilhelm Niesel and Peter Brunner. In addition, the writings of nineteenth-century conservative theologians were again read. The work of the Dutch theologian Hermann Friedrich Kohlbrügge (1803–1875), with its stress on the sovereignty of God's grace in salvation, was especially important to Barth.

Study of the Reformation confessions was also resumed by some. Barth prepared a report for the World Presbyterian Alliance meeting held in Cardiff, Wales, in June and July, 1925. The paper was entitled "The Desirability and Possibility of a General Reformed Confession of Faith."

After presenting nine characteristics of a genuine Reformed confession, Barth expressed grave doubts about the possibility of a true confession at that time.

> Where has there been in the theology of our time the erection of a great truth by which the Church felt itself seriously claimed or of a great heresy by which it felt itself gravely and intolerably attacked? Where is there an Athanasius, a Luther among us, not to speak of phenomena like an Augustine, a Thomas, and a Calvin who were not only stimulating and moving but who also shaped the movements they founded? What would be the special cause to which the church would have to bear public witness today?

The dialectical theologians were initially united by reaction against their liberal background. Soon there developed internal debates among the contributors to *Zwischen den Zeiten*. Barth's thinking became increasingly concentrated on Christ as the center of his theology. He continually strove to eliminate anthropological or philosophical elements. Rudolf Bultmann increasingly opposed him, leading Barth to ask whether for Bultmann "theology and anthropology were really interchangeable concepts." Emil Brunner developed, in opposition to Barth, his own theology which emphasized a "point of contact" for God's revelation in human reason.

Before March 1933, Barth regarded the protests of Gogarten, Bultmann, and Brunner as intramural arguments which would not divide the church. With the rise of the "German Christians," however, Barth increasingly viewed his colleagues' positions as dangerous heresies. In March, the "dialectical school" broke up. Gogarten joined the "German Christians" (withdrawing, however, in November 1933). Barth resigned from the editorial board of *Zwischen den Zeiten*. Brunner, who remained in Switzerland, was not personally involved in the political controversy. Barth was angered, however, because Brunner's debates with him won loud applause from German theologians, such as Otto Weber and Paul Althaus, who were sympathetic to the "German Christians."

The Confessing Church

On January 11, 1933, a group of twenty-one pastors met at Altona in reaction to the "German Christians" movement and issued a declaration entitled "A Word and Confession to the Need and Confusion in Public Life." This document noted that many people were asking about the nature of the church. Dr. Hans Asmussen, leader of the group, viewed the church's responsibility as that of sharpening the conscience and proclaiming the gospel.

Three weeks later, on January 30, 1933, Adolf Hitler became Chancellor. Hitler used the burning of the Reichstag building on February 27 as an excuse for issuing an emergency order which virtually abolished civil rights. On March 5, the new elections Hitler had called gave him 44 percent of the vote and a near majority in the Reichstag. On March 23, 1933, in a speech before the first meeting of the Reichstag, he declared:

> The national Government . . . will respect the agreements that have been drawn up between [the churches] and the provincial states. Their rights are not to be infringed. It expects, however, and hopes that conversely the work upon the national and moral renewal of our nation, which the Government has assumed as its task, will receive the same appreciation. All denominations will be treated with the same impartial justice. . . .
>
> The Reich Government, seeing in Christianity the unshakable foundation of the moral and ethical life of our people, attaches utmost importance to the cultivation and shaping of the friendliest relations with the Holy See.

> The rights of the churches will not be curtailed: their position in relation to the State will not be changed.

On April 3–5, 1933, in Berlin the "German Christians" had their first national convention. Its slogan was "The State of Adolf Hitler appeals to the Church and the Church has to hear his call." Among the members of the honorary committee were high-ranking governmental officials and Nazi party members, including Hermann Göring. The convention closed by passing a resolution which stated:

> God has created me a German. Germanism is a gift of God. God wants me to fight for my Germany. Military service is in no sense a violation of Christian conscience, but is obedience to God. The believer possesses the right of revolution against a State that furthers the powers of darkness. He also has this right in the face of a Church board that does not unreservedly acknowledge the exaltation of the nation. For a German the church is the fellowship of believers who are obligated to fight for a Christian Germany. The goal of the "Faith Movement of 'German Christians'" is an evangelical German Reich Church.

The Reich (National) Church

With the appointment in April 1933 of a State Commissioner for the Evangelical Church in Mecklenburg, it appeared that Hitler had not kept his promise of not interfering with the churches. On April 25, Hitler, fearing overzealousness from the radical wing of the "German Christians," appointed Ludwig Müller, a moderate, as his confidential adviser and deputy in church affairs. Hitler charged him with the responsibility of creating a Reich Church. Müller, a man in his fifties, had spent most of his career as a chaplain serving in naval and military units in East Prussia. He was a fervent Nazi, an ardent admirer of Hitler, and a leader of the "German Christians." "I am to see to it that the struggle for the future of the evangelical Church will not be conducted like the political struggle," Müller said, and read a statement to the press:

> The goal is the fulfillment of the longing of evangelical Germans since the time of the Reformation. The situation . . . is as follows: the "German Christians" want an evangelical German Reich Church. They have stirred up the Church people. The Church administrations also want a great "Evangelical Church of the German Nation." This Church is now to be built. The Reformation Confessions of our fathers will point us the way. . . . In the name of the Reich Chancellor, I call upon all concerned to engage in honest co-operation. May the Lord of the Church grant us the Spirit of unanimity, that together we may set to work with complete confidence.

Hermann Kapler, president of the German Evangelical Church Federation was authorized to take the necessary steps to write a new church constitution on the basis of existing Confessions of Faith. With Bishop August Marahrens and Dr. Hermann Albert Hesse assisting him, he initiated the actions that were to lead to the publication of the constitution of the German Evangelical Church, which was accepted by State Law on July 14, 1933. Essentially, this unified under one national church all the Protestant churches and religious organizations. The law was signed by Hitler and by Minister for Internal Affairs Wilhelm Frick. The first article of the constitution read, "The inviolable foundation of the German Evangelical Church is the gospel of Jesus Christ as it is attested for us in Holy Scripture and brought to light again in the Confessions of the Reformation. The full powers that the Church needs for its mission are thereby determined and limited." On the same day, Hitler outlawed all political parties except the National Socialist Party.

Following the ratification of the German Evangelical Church Constitution, there came a complex power play culminating in the "German Christians'" gaining control of the Reich Church. Church elections were announced and set for July 26. However, rather than being democratic elections, they turned out to be a mass Nazi propaganda campaign. On the eve of the election, Hitler spoke on nationwide radio urging support of the "German Christians" movement. The result was a resounding victory for the "German Christians" party.

President Paul von Hindenberg died on August 2, 1934. Hitler then abolished the presidency and proclaimed himself *Reichsführer* (National Leader) as well as Chancellor. All military and governmental officials were compelled to take an unconditional oath of personal allegiance to Hitler.

On August 4, the Church Senate of the Prussian Church, the largest of the *Landeskirchen* (regional churches), elected Müller president of the consistory, with the title of Bishop. At the National Synod held in Wittenberg on September 27, he was elected Reich Bishop. In his acceptance speech Müller declared:

> The whole German movement is for us a present from God given in a time when the enemies of Christianity are doing their best to destroy our people. . . . The old has passed away. The new has emerged. The church's struggle is passed. Now begins the struggle for the soul of the people.

Müller presided at the General Synod of the Prussian Church which convened on September 4, one day after the Reich Party Congress was held in Nuremberg under the slogan, "Triumph of Faith." With the laws passed at this synod, the assimilation of the largest of the *Landeskirchen* to the state was accomplished. It was here that Karl Koch, chairman of the "Gospel and Church" minority group, was shouted down as he tried to read a statement of protest regarding the secular principles and methods being introduced into the church.

The Pastors' Emergency League

Following the Prussian General Synod, Martin Niemoeller, pastor of the Lutheran Berlin-Dahlem congregation, established the Pastors' Emergency League. Niemoeller sent a circular letter to all German pastors on September 21, 1933. It stated:

> Because of this need we have formed an "Emergency League" of ministers who have given written assurance to one another that in their preaching they will be bound only by Holy Scripture and the Confessions of the Reformation and to the best of their ability will succor those brethren who in doing so have to suffer.

The immediate response to Niemoeller's letter exceeded all expectations; 1,300 signed up. By the end of September the number had grown to 2,300. By January 1934 there were over seven thousand members.

The Berlin Sport Palace demonstration, staged by the "German Christians" on November 13, provoked a storm of indignation and protest and gave the Pastors' Emergency League its first major chance to act. The purpose of this demonstration was to rekindle the fighting spirit of the movement and to place again in the forefront the old goals of the "German Christians." Dr. Reinhold Krause delivered an inflammatory speech to 20,000 participants in which he stated that the German Reformation begun by Luther would be completed in the Third Reich by the formation of a new church, a "mighty, new, all-embracing German national Church." The first step in the creation of a new indigenous church, according to Krause, was to get rid of "the Old Testament with its Jewish morality of rewards, and its stories of cattle dealers and panders." The New Testament was to be purged of all superstitious passages, including the whole theology of the Rabbi Paul with its ideas of scapegoats and its sense of inferiority. An exaggerated view of the Crucified was to be avoided and a "heroic" Jesus proclaimed. Krause's speech was punctuated by enthusiastic applause, and at its conclusion he received a standing ovation. The meeting concluded with passage of a resolution reflecting Krause's views and demanding the discharge of ministers who were not willing to cooperate in the new Reformation in the spirit of National Socialism.

The first to protest this outrage were three leaders of the Pastors' Emergency League, Martin and Wilhelm Niemoeller and Gerhard Jacobi. They demanded that Müller immediately denounce Krause. On the following Sunday, November 19, 1933, 3,000 members of the League read from their pulpits a denunciation of the church government. The National Socialist Party leaders were annoyed by the unrest and issued a declaration of strict neutrality in religious disputes. This furor resulted in a withdrawal of support from the "German Christians" movement by Müller, as Hitler's puppet. Since the "German Christians" movement was no longer necessary to the Nazi party, it was ignored.

In response to this confusing and uncertain situation, the First Free Reformed Synod met in Barmen-Gemarke on January 3 and 4, 1934. Martin Niemoeller was among the 320 elders and ministers present. Following two statements issued the previous year, Karl Barth drew up a "Declaration Concerning the Right Understanding of the Reformation Confessions of Faith in the German Evangelical Church of the Present." The document was promptly endorsed. It marked the first anti-Nazi confession by a church body rather than an individual theologian or group of theologians. Although it was a declaration by a Reformed Synod, it strove to speak on behalf of the one Evangelical Church of Jesus Christ in the face of common error.

On January 4, 1934, Reich Bishop Müller issued a "Muzzling Order," which forbade any public criticism of church administration or discussion of church controversy. Once again the Pastors' Emergency League responded with a wave of protests, read in nearly 4,000 churches.

Church Leaders' Meeting with Hitler

At the same time, Müller was being attacked by his banished "German Christian" supporters. In an attempt to save the discredited Müller and stifle unwelcome press comment in the rest of the world, Hitler decided to intervene. He summoned about forty prominent church leaders to the Reich Chancellery on January 25. With Müller at his side, Hitler began the meeting by reading a prepared statement. After only a few lines, he was rudely interrupted by Göring, who created dissension by describing a tapped phone conversation between Niemoeller and Walther Künneth, co-chairman of the Young Reformation Movement. Hitler exploded in rage at the information Göring related. Niemoeller tried to explain, to which Hitler replied, "You leave the care of the Third Reich to me and you look after the church." Göring further agitated the situation by claiming that the Pastors' Emergency League had "foreign connections." As the clergymen were leaving, Niemoeller addressed Hitler:

> *Herr Reichskanzler,* you said just now, "I will take care of the German people." But we too as Christians and churchmen have a responsibility toward the German people. That responsibility was entrusted to us by God, and neither you nor anyone in this world has the power to take it from us.

The morning of January 26, 1934, was a dark one for Martin Niemoeller. All but one of the clergymen who had been in attendance with him in Hitler's office felt that his outspokenness had ruined their only chance to patch up things with the Führer. They drew up a condemnation of Niemoeller and withdrew en masse from the Pastors' Emergency League. This came as a severe blow to Niemoeller, who had expected that the other members would back him in his stand against Hitler's policies.

Events Leading to the Synod of Barmen

Over the next few months there was no effective compromise, and the power of Reich Bishop Müller continued to grow. In April, Dr. August Jäger, a man of anti-Christian convictions, was appointed Legal Administrator of the Reich Church. Many saw this as an obvious move by Hitler to subvert the church and assimilate it into the government. On April 22, 1934, the leaders of the Pastors' Emergency League formed the Constitutional Evangelical Church of Germany and declared it to be the true church within the German Evangelical Church. The leaders of the Pastors' Emergency League, who were called the Council of Brethren, called a synod of the Constitutional Evangelical Church for the end of May, 1934. They appointed a committee to handle the theological preparation for the synod, which was to be held in Barmen. This committee was composed of three men: Hans Asmussen, Thomas Breit, and Karl Barth.

By now, the leaders of the Pastors' Emergency League knew that there could be no compromise with the "German Christians" or the Nazi regime. The church government was based on arbitrary power instead of law. It was injuring the Confession of Faith instead of defending it, and was opposing the Confessing Church, not the enemies of the faith. The first declaration which the committee wrote stated that the church had to stand for the confessions of the Reformation. They insisted that the unity of the Evangelical Churches in Germany could only come from the Word of God in faith through the Holy Spirit. This opposed the attempts to establish the unity of the German Evangelical Church by means of false doctrine, force, and insincere practices.

They set the date of the Barmen Synod for May 29–31, 1934. Asmussen, Breit, and Barth went to work on the document to be presented. They drew heavily upon Holy Scripture, confessions of the Reformation, "A Word and Confession to the Need and Confusion in Public Life" (from a conference in Altona in January 1933), and the "Declaration Concerning the Right Understanding of the Reformation Confessions of Faith in the German Evangelical Church of the Present" from the First Free Reformed Synod at Barmen in January 1934.

Asmussen, Breit, and Barth met and discussed the essential aspects of what such a document should include. They proceeded from Articles 1 and 4 of the constitution of the German Evangelical Church. Article 1 stated that the basis of the German Evangelical Church was the gospel of Jesus Christ as it was set forth in Scripture and in the confessions of the Reformation. Article 4 related the fulfillment of the divine mission of the church. The presupposition of their discussion was that this legal basis of the constitution had been broken by the Reich Church and Reich government. Considering that the question of the structure of the Evangelical Church was really one of its confession, they felt it necessary to take a position regarding the source of revelation, justification, and sanctification.

For Asmussen the solution had to be based on a theological stand. Breit cautioned that it could not legally be a confessional declaration because they were starting from the constitution of the German Evangelical Church and there was no particular confession therein. Their purpose, as Barth saw it, was not to create a church union; rather, it was a matter of three churches—Lutheran, Reformed, and United—confessing their faith on the basis of the ancient confessions in the face of existing concrete errors.

It was a hot afternoon, and the committee members had taken wine with their lunch. Accordingly, they decided on a short nap before resuming work. However, unable to sleep, Barth began to work on the first draft of the document. This draft became the original form of the Barmen Declaration. Asmussen wrote an additional commentary, thus completing the work of the committee.

The Synod at Barmen convened on the evening of May 29, 1934. The delegates represented a considerable variety of geographical, denominational, and theological backgrounds. Overall it was a rather youthful gathering; the average age of the delegates was under forty. Karl Barth's official invitation to the synod was nearly overlooked. Only two days before the synod began, someone discovered this oversight and the president, Dr. Karl Koch, personally telegraphed Barth, requesting him to come. On the floor of the meeting, Barth did not speak, leaving it to Hans Asmussen to speak for the theological committee.

On the morning of May 30, 1934, the Barmen Declaration was passed out to the delegates. Asmussen addressed the gathering in support of the document. An expanded theological commission composed of eight members, chaired by Breit, was appointed. They edited and revised the Declaration to the satisfaction of the synod. On May 31, the synod unanimously adopted the Declaration. The delegates responded by singing the last stanza of "Now Thank We All Our God."

By clarifying its faith in the words of the Barmen Declaration, a minority within the Evangelical Church of Germany had reconstituted itself as a "Confessing Church." The idolatry of the "German Christians" in giving an ultimate commitment to the state rather than God was recognized as error. Jesus Christ, as attested in Scripture, was proclaimed as the one Word of God and Lord of all life. The Declaration became the basis for the subsequent synods of Dahlem in 1934, Augsburg in 1935, and Bad-Oeynhausen in 1936. It provided the theological basis for the Confessing Church in its stand against the Hitler regime throughout the war. Following the war, the Declaration gave guidance for the Confession of Stuttgart, in which the German church acknowledged its own guilt for the atrocities committed against the Jews and others by the Nazi state.

In an evaluation of the function of the Barmen Declaration after the war, Karl Barth, its chief author, stressed both its limitations and its value. He noted that no other major institution had offered significant resistance to the Nazi menace—not the universities, the legal profession, business, the arts, the army, or the trade unions. He then commented about the Barmen Declaration of the Confessing Church:

> Even it was not a total resistance against totalitarian National Socialism. It restricted itself to repelling the encroachment of National Socialism. It confined itself to the Church's Confession, to the Church service, and to Church order as such. It was only a partial resistance. And for this it has been properly and improperly reproached. . . . In proportion to its task, the church has sufficient reason to be ashamed that it did not do more; yet in comparison with those other groups and institutions it has no reason to be ashamed; it accomplished far more than all the rest.

Essential Tenets of the Reformed Faith

The Sin of Idolatry

In Reformed theology, atheism is not the problem. Idolatry is. The Reformed faith has argued, with Calvin, following Augustine, that every person knows God. That knowledge, implanted in all human hearts, is suppressed by human sin. People choose not to acknowledge God as their creator, and so they create idols. An idol is any humanly created thing to which people give their ultimate allegiance. Idolatry is giving our total commitment to something in the creation rather than to the Creator alone. Israel was not troubled by lack of belief in God. The people of God have always been tempted to worship other gods, which in reality are not gods at all. In our modern world, they are not small figures of animals and humans made of wood, clay, and stone. But when we put our worldly possessions, our family status, or our national honor above our allegiance to God, then that is idolatry.

The Theological Declaration of Barmen responded to the errors of the "German Christians" by confessing six evangelical truths. In each case, a passage from Scripture was offered, a theological affirmation was made, and an error of the "German Christians" was rejected. The last four of the six statements were directed against the idolatry of giving ultimate loyalty to any idea, person, institution, or purpose. In a litany, beginning in each case with "We reject the false doctrine," the Theological Declaration pointed to four forms of idolatry: "prevailing ideological and political convictions . . . ; special leaders vested with ruling powers . . . ; as though the State, over and beyond its special commission, should and could become the single and totalitarian order of human life, thus fulfilling the Church's vocation as well . . . ; as though the Church in human arrogance could place the Word and work of the Lord in the service of any arbitrarily chosen desires, purposes, and plans."

The Barmen Declaration is especially careful not to refer to the state as an "order" or an "order of existence." This is the language about government found in the articles of the "German Christians." An "order" in this context implied a structure established by God which was above criticism in its nature, if not in its actions. Article 5 of the Theological Declaration of Barmen begins with the bold quotation, "'*Fear God. Honor the emperor.*' (I Peter 2:17.)" The church honors government. The attitude expressed here is the same as that in the Scots Confession: obey legitimate government, but resist illegitimate tyranny. In the Barmen Declaration, not the order of the state but its *task* is primary. The state "has by divine appointment the task of providing for justice and peace." The Declaration therefore rejects the false doctrine, "as though the State, over and beyond its special commission, should and could become the single and totalitarian order of human life, thus fulfilling the Church's vocation as well."

The Theological Declaration of Barmen is characteristically Reformed in its polemic against idolatry. This iconoclasm (breaking of idols) marked the attitude of ancient Israel. It was manifested in the earliest Reformed communities, beginning with Zwingli's purification of the church in Zürich, and was carried on by the Puritans. It has as its basis the strong Reformed reaction to putting anything in the place of God in our worship. Not only in church but in the world, the Reformed tradition has always attempted to honor God as the Lord of all life. A biographer of John Knox reflected that the best servants of the state are those whose highest loyalty is not to the state but to God. When humans attempt to fulfill their deepest desires for meaning in anything other than God the Creator, they commit idolatry. When human beings put their trust in the work of human hands rather than the Creator, they end up, as the Nazis did, by destroying humanity.

The Lordship of Jesus Christ

The evangelical affirmations of the Theological Declaration of Barmen all center on the Lordship of Jesus Christ. Jesus Christ, declared in the Nicene Creed to be both divine and human in one integral person, was, at Barmen, proclaimed to be the one Word, or revelation, of God, to the church and to the world.

Article 1 states: "Jesus Christ, as he is attested for us in Holy Scripture, is the one Word of God which we have to hear and which we have to trust and obey in life and in death." This was a clear rejection of "natural theology," the notion that a person, without the revelation of Christ in

Scripture, can discern in nature or history the purpose and plan of God.

Some German theologians had welcomed Hitler's rise to power as "a gift and miracle of God." The "German Christians" announced, as a guiding principle, "We see in race, folk, and nation, orders of existence granted and entrusted to us by God," and they proceeded to use that principle to argue against German citizenship for Jews. The Theological Declaration of Barmen rejects as false doctrine any revelation in "other events and powers, figures and truths," besides "this one Word of God," Jesus Christ, as attested in Scripture.

Article 2 affirms that Jesus Christ "is God's assurance of the forgiveness of all our sins." Following that word of personal comfort, the Barmen Declaration continues, saying, "with the same seriousness he is also God's mighty claim upon our whole life." The first affirmation is that we are justified by God's grace in Jesus Christ. The second affirmation is that God desires that we be sanctified, that we grow in acknowledgment of Christ's claim on all of our life.

This article is true to the Reformed background of its author, Karl Barth. The German Lutherans traditionally were comfortable with a doctrine of "two kingdoms." This concept was rooted in Luther's indebtedness for protection to the German princes; it allowed that there was one kingdom of the church, which was of the spirit and therefore a private realm, and another kingdom of the state, which was of the world, a public realm. The two were separate and had no claim on each other. The Barmen Declaration rejects this "two kingdom" theory as false doctrine, "as though there were areas of our life in which we would not belong to Jesus Christ, but to other lords—areas in which we would not need justification and sanctification through him."

Article 3 defines the Christian church as "the congregation of the brethren in which Jesus Christ acts presently as the Lord in Word and sacrament through the Holy Spirit." This does not make church members especially holy or exempt from problems. Rather, the church is composed of "pardoned sinners" who have to "testify in the midst of a sinful world." But the message of the church, expressed in faith and obedience, is that "it is solely his [Christ's] property." The church "lives and wants to live solely from his comfort and from his direction in the expectation of his appearance."

The word "comfort" here reminds us of the same word used in the first question and answer of the Heidelberg Catechism. Comfort, in the Reformed theological sense, means "strength." It comes from the Latin *fortis,* as in "A mighty fortress is our God." The comfort which Christ gives is not ease and an absence of problems. God in Christ gives us strength to meet whatever problems we have to encounter in the world. The Theological Declaration of Barmen, in Article 3, therefore rejects the false doctrine, "as though the Church were permitted to abandon the form of its message and order to its own pleasure or to changes in prevailing ideological and political convictions." Reformed theology declares that there is no comfort in conforming to the world. Only in reliance on the Lordship of Jesus Christ is there strength.

Contemporary Relevance

Idolatry in a Democracy?

One of the most memorable figures in the struggle of the Confessing Church against Hitler was Pastor Martin Niemoeller, who died in 1984 at the age of ninety-two. He had been a German U-boat commander in World War I and was known as the Scourge of Malta. After the war, he studied theology and became a Lutheran pastor, moving in 1931 to the influential Dahlem parish in Berlin. There, as we have seen, he organized the Pastors' Emergency

League. And there he continued publicly to oppose Hitler until the Gestapo seized him in 1937. He spent seven years in concentration camps.

Martin Niemoeller was an intensely patriotic man. During the early years of the Nazi regime he organized the Academic Defense Corps, an armed student nationalist organization. In 1939, from prison, Niemoeller volunteered to reenlist in the submarine corps. He explained later that his sons were fighting and risking death, and he wished to stand with them. Though Niemoeller was one of the first church leaders to speak out against the Nazis, after the war he was willing to share the guilt of his people. Speaking for all those who could have done more, he said,

> In Germany they came first for the communists, and I didn't speak up because I wasn't a communist. Then they came for the Jews, and I didn't speak up because I wasn't a Jew. Then they came for the trade unionists, and I didn't speak up because I wasn't a trade unionist. Then they came for the Catholics, and I didn't speak up because I was a Protestant. Then they came for me, and by that time no one was left to speak up.

After his release from Dachau in October 1945, Niemoeller preached before a gathering of German church leaders and representatives of the ecumenical movement. His message was, "We have no right to pass off all guilt on the evil Nazis. . . . We the church failed." The Stuttgart Declaration expressed that need for repentance and the affirmation: "Now a new beginning is to be made in our churches."

Niemoeller's dedication to that new beginning took him to Moscow in 1952 for conversations with Russian Orthodox Church leaders. He was a founder, and later one of the presidents, of the World Council of Churches. He opposed the remilitarization of Germany. At the age of eighty-nine he marched with 70,000 others in Hamburg to protest the arms race. He was often criticized in his own country and elsewhere for his pacifism. "Live according to the Gospel without fear, or fail" was one of his favorite admonitions.

As Reformed Christians we must always ask ourselves how clear our understanding is of the potential threat of idolatry in our own time and place. At the 1984 General Assembly of the Presbyterian Church (U.S.A.), Dr. Arnold B. Come, retired president of San Francisco Theological Seminary, spoke to the theme of the application of the Theological Declaration of Barmen today. He asked his audience of over a thousand Presbyterians:

> What would you do if your government were trying to dictate where and when and what your children might pray and, by amending the Constitution and by the power of taxation, to determine how you shall act in matters reserved for the privacy of your Christian conscience? What would you do if the leader of your government were declaring that the American way of life and values are the truly Godly and Christian ways and values, and that other nations and their governments are the instrument of the devil? What would you do if you were condemned as anti-Christian when you raised your voice in criticism of some of our American values and the military exploits and armament policies of our government?

Come observed that the true confession of the members of the Confessing Church "took place in the decisions of their hearts and in the deeds of their daily lives." He quoted the reaction of Albert Einstein to the witness of the Confessing Church of the Barmen Declaration: "Only the church stood squarely across the path of Hitler's campaign for suppressing the truth. . . . I am forced to confess that what I once despised, I now praise unreservedly."

The Transformation of Culture

Culture, in the language of anthropologists, is the total nonbiologically transmitted heritage of the human race. Culture does not refer just to sophisticated aspects of life such as art and music. Humans are in culture as fish are in water. Culture conditions the way in which we respond to reality. Every culture has a worldview, a set of assumptions enabling people to make sense out of life and integrate their experiences. During Christian history there have been a number of different ways that the church has related to the surrounding culture. Accompanying these different modes of adaptation have been different theories about the proper relationship of the Christian faith to the general culture.

During the first three centuries of its existence, the Christian church was seen as a threat to the pretensions to lordship of the Roman emperors. The church was persecuted as a countercultural force. In the fourth century, when the Emperor Constantine became a Christian, the church was first tolerated and then favored. Under Constantine's son, Theodosius, the empire became officially Christian. This attitude prevailed into the Middle Ages, during which Europe was considered to be a Christian culture.

The Protestant Reformers did not explicitly reject the notion of a Christian society, with every person living in a certain parish area as officially related to the church in that place. But Calvin and others knew that in reality Christendom was an illusion. Rather than discarding the concept, Calvin sought to make the Lordship of Christ genuinely effective in the city of Geneva. His first efforts led to his being thrown out of town. But upon observing the alternatives, the city leaders invited him back, and Geneva became, in the words of John Knox, "the most perfect school of Christ that ever was on earth since the days of the Apostles."

Some Americans yearn for a return to the status of a Christian society that they believe the Middle Ages embodied. Others claim that the Reformers shared that vision and made it work in the sixteenth century. Writers eloquently describe the founding of the United States of America in terms of a Christian society which they believe has been diminished or lost in recent years.

Several factors have been at work, ever since the thirteenth century, which have radically changed the relationship between Christianity and culture. These factors were all strongly present in the early years of the American nation and seem unlikely to be reversed. First is the secularization of society. The state is now officially secular, and the institutions of society meeting human needs, such as medicine, education, and science, are no longer controlled by the church. Second, the church is fragmented into a plurality of denominations. That was an outgrowth of the revivalism which swept eighteenth-century America and of the suspicion of the state Church of England which helped to motivate the American revolution. Third, religious freedom is prized and institutionalized in the Constitutional provision for the separation of church and state. This freedom made possible the frontier revivals of the nineteenth century and has yielded a condition where America has the highest percentage of its people attending church of any nation in the world.

What are our options as Reformed Christians for acting out the Lordship of Christ in the present cultural situation? The now-classic study of H. Richard Niebuhr, *Christ and Culture,* presented a variety of approaches that Christians have most often taken. Anthropologist Charles H. Kraft has responded to and further developed this variety in his book *Christianity in Culture.* He notes three approaches that have had significant influence in American church life. All three have tried to honor the fact that Christ is both above and yet within culture, the Christ is in some sense in opposition to and yet in another sense in agreement with human culture. These three positions differ in their emphases.

First is the position that emphasizes a Christ *of* culture. This was the view of Thomas Aquinas and the medieval Roman Catholic Church. Niebuhr labels them *synthesists.* Christianity and culture are synthesized, or identified. Christ fulfills cultural aspirations and permeates the institutions of society. The danger of this view is that it easily slips over into Christ *endorsing* culture. People declare that their culture is the only Christian way in which human life can be organized and lived.

Second is the view that emphasizes Christ *against* culture. This is the attitude of people such as Roger Williams and the more extreme Anabaptists and, to some extent, Martin Luther. Niebuhr calls them *dualists.* Christianity and society are sharply divided. There is a basic conflict between the righteousness of God and the manner in which humans as such live. The only solution to this problem is for Christians to *withdraw* from the general society and create their own counterculture based on strict Christian discipline.

Third is the stance that emphasizes a Christ *transforming* culture. Augustine, Calvin, and, in some ways, Charles Wesley are examples of this attitude. Niebuhr's name for them is *conversionists.* God is transcendent (above) human culture, but God is also, since the incarnation of Jesus Christ, immanent (within) human affairs. The task of Christianity is to *transform* sinful human culture and its institutions from within. Reformed believers are not deluded into thinking that human society can be perfected and made wholly Christian. However, in obedience to God they accept the effort to make the institutions of this world more conformed to God's will for the good of all.

In the 1980s some interesting shifts in religious attitudes have taken place. Fundamentalist Christians who traditionally took the Anabaptist attitude of Christ *against* culture have now changed dramatically. Since the bicentennial, strong currents of American patriotism have been blended with conservative religious beliefs. Especially since the 1980 presidential election, many fundamentalists have shifted to a stance of Christ *endorsing* culture. America is seen as God's chosen nation with a special calling from God to Christianize the world and make American governmental and economic institutions the norm for all. The adherence to particular political programs of, for example, the Moral Majority has been used as a yardstick by which to judge the Christian commitment of candidates for public office and members of Congress.

Reformed Christians will usually remain unsatisfied with the one-sided solutions of either the far right or the far left. America is not a Christian nation, nor is it likely to become one by the election of a particular president or the dominance of a single party. Neither is America without any virtue, so that we should give up on it and retreat into some sort of countercultural enclave. Presbyterians will continue to study the issues, to vote, to run for office, and to use every legitimate means to influence the political process. We will not achieve the kingdom of God on earth. We can, however, remain faithful to our Lord and to the task of transforming culture. The Theological Declaration of Barmen constantly reminds us that no human being or institution is divinely ordained to have ultimate authority in our lives. No human ruler or party may be followed uncritically. Only Jesus Christ is the Lord of the church, and of all life.

10

The Confession of 1967

The most recently drafted document in *The Book of Confessions* is the Confession of 1967. To members of the former United Presbyterian Church in the U.S.A., it is perhaps the best known and most widely used. The former Presbyterian Church in the U.S. produced "A Declaration of Faith" in 1976. It was adopted by the 1977 General Assembly, but the *Book of Confessions* of which it was a part did not receive enough votes in the presbyteries to become a part of the constitution. "A Declaration of Faith" was, however, widely used in worship and study in the former PCUS.

The Confession of 1967 represented a confirmation of the lasting values of the New Reformation theology initiated in Europe by Karl Barth and others and further developed in American beginning in the 1930s. The Confession of 1967 also marked the culmination of over thirty years of relative theological homogeneity which had prevailed in the church following the disruptions caused by the fundamentalist/modernist controversies of the 1920s. Seminary instruction, church school curriculum, and denominational policy-making had all drawn on the same theological resources during the 1930s, 1940s, and 1950s. That vital consensus was made confessional in the Confession of 1967 just before the working agreements on theological methodology in America began to fragment in the late 1960s and the present era of theological pluralism began.

The Confession of 1967 also constituted a new beginning in the expression of Reformed confessional statements. All the creeds, confessions, and declarations of the Reformed tradition arose in the context of social and political controversy. Each of these implicitly addressed the issues of their time in ways which the authors and original recipients understood. But the Confession of 1967 was the first Reformed statement overtly and explicitly to name and confront current social problems of its own era. Thus the Confession of 1967 provided the church with a clear theological orientation by which to meet central social issues of the 1960s and 1970s.

In 1982, a symposium, "The Confession of 1967: Contemporary Implications," was attended by some two hundred Presbyterians at Princeton Theological Seminary. The symposium celebrated fifteen years of service by the confession. Participants addressed, among other issues, the manner in which the theme of reconciliation in the Confession of 1967 had supported and enabled Presbyterians to respond positively to the theological motif of liberation which rose to prominence in the 1970s.

Historical Context: The Case of the Confession of 1967

Edward A. Dowey, Jr., gathered his notes, walked to the podium, and stood facing the members of the Committee on Bills and Overtures. It was May 1967. In the midst of the 179th General Assembly of The United Presbyterian Church in the U.S.A., debate had erupted regarding the constitutionality of the proposed Confession of 1967. As chair of the committee charged to prepare the confession, Dowey had spent nearly nine years on its development and that of the *Book of Confessions* of which it was a part.

Seven years of research and writing had preceded presentation of the initial draft of the Confession of 1967 to the General Assembly in 1965. That had been followed by a year of study throughout the denomination and by revisions made by a Special Committee of Fifteen. The revised document had been approved by the 178th General Assembly in 1966 and submitted to the presbyteries. The new *Book of Confessions,* including the Confession of 1967, had garnered more than the two-thirds approval necessary to change the constitution. Now all that remained to complete the constitutional process was an affirmative vote of the 1967 General Assembly. But just as final approval hovered in the wings, a new snag had threatened to disrupt completion of the task.

The Book of Confessions, of which the Confession of 1967 was a part, included the ancient Nicene and Apostles' creeds; three sixteenth-century statements, the Scots Confession, the Heidelberg Catechism, and the Second Helvetic Confession; and the Theological Declaration of Barmen. It also incorporated the traditional doctrinal standards of American Presbyterianism, the Westminster Confession of Faith and the Shorter Catechism. The lengthy and seldom-used Larger Catechism, however, was omitted.

Four presbyteries had submitted overtures questioning the constitutionality of the entire procedure under which the change in the confessional position had been made. The basis for the complaint was that while the constitution of the denomination provided for "amending" or "altering" the subordinate standards, it did not provide for "deleting." Proponents of the overtures argued that deletion of the Larger Catechism rendered the whole process of confessional revision unconstitutional and therefore invalid.

As he prepared to speak to the Bills and Overtures Committee, Dowey felt sure that it was both legal and wise to omit the Larger Catechism. There were precedents for dropping subordinate standards. The theological material in the Larger Catechism was also present in the Westminster Confession and the Shorter Catechism. And hardly anyone ever read the Larger Catechism any more. Dowey believed firmly that confessions should be not just monuments to the past but relevant tools for the present mission of the church. Would his arguments convince the committee?

Debates Over Doctrine

The transition to the twentieth century in America was marked by signs of growing theological turmoil. The evolutionary theories of Charles Darwin, the development of "biblical criticism," and the rise of industrialism rocked the churches—and the Presbyterian Church was not exempt. One of the early storm warnings came when Dr. Charles A. Briggs, a Presbyterian professor at Union Theological Seminary in New York, was forced to resign from the ministry in 1893. The General Assembly declared that his rejection of the theory of biblical inerrancy and his sympathies with the new "higher criticism" made his views on the Bible incompatible with the Westminster Confession of Faith.

The Briggs case became the springboard for decades of conflict in the Presbyterian Church. In 1910, the General Assembly adopted a five-point declaration of "essential and necessary doctrines" which all candidates for ordination had to affirm. These points began with (1) the inerrancy of the Bible. The other four points in order were (2) the virgin birth of Christ, (3) Christ's substitutionary atonement, (4) Christ's bodily resurrection, and (5) the authenticity of Christ's mighty miracles. This five-point creed-within-a-creed was reaffirmed by the Presbyterian General Assemblies of 1916 and 1923.

Other Christian groups picked up the five points and refashioned them for their own use. Often point number two became the deity of Christ rather than his virgin birth.

Many lists concluded with Christ's premillennial second coming instead of his miracles, as point number five. This was especially true for the growing movement of independent Bible conferences, Bible schools, and independent churches influenced by Dispensationalism. This movement majored in literalistic, futuristic interpretation of biblical prophecy which announced Christ's imminent return following a very specific and complex timetable of attendant events. Dispensationalists also taught that all the traditional institutional churches had grown worldly and denied fundamental doctrinal beliefs. By the 1920s, the five points of the Presbyterians had been transformed into the "five fundamentals" and had become a rallying point for conservative Christians across a broad spectrum.

In May 1922, Harry Emerson Fosdick preached a sermon in the First Presbyterian Church in New York City entitled "Shall the Fundamentalists Win?" It followed a debate in *The New York Times* with William Jennings Bryan over the matter of teaching evolution in the public schools. Clarence Edward Macartney, pastor of the Arch Street Presbyterian Church in Philadelphia, responded to Fosdick with the sermon "Shall Unbelief Win?" In 1923, Bryan was narrowly defeated as the conservative candidate for Moderator of the General Assembly. But Bryan and Macartney persuaded the Assembly to instruct the Presbytery of New York to take corrective action regarding the pulpit at First Presbyterian. Also in 1923, a book appeared entitled *Christianity and Liberalism* written by J. Gresham Machen, a professor at Princeton Theological Seminary. According to Machen, liberalism was "un-Christian," a different religion from Christianity. "A separation between the two parties in the Church is the crying need of the hour," he declared.

In 1924, 13 percent of the ministers in the Presbyterian Church signed a document called the Auburn Affirmation. It argued that the five points, or fundamentals, which the General Assembly had reaffirmed the previous year were theories that went beyond the facts to which Scripture and the Westminster Confession obligated them. However, at the General Assembly of 1924, William Jennings Bryan nominated Macartney, who was narrowly elected Moderator, and actions of the Assembly finally forced Fosdick to resign from First Presbyterian in 1925.

By this time there were three identifiable political parties within the Presbyterian Church. One was composed of theological liberals, who believed in an inclusive church, containing any who wished to belong. Opposed to them were doctrinal fundamentalists, who argued for an exclusivist church composed only of those who agreed with the five fundamental points. The largest group, though least well organized, was made up of moderates, who were theologically conservative but were inclusivists for the sake of the peace, unity, and mission of the church. The General Assembly in 1925 elected a moderate, Charles R. Erdman, professor of practical theology at Princeton, as Moderator. Erdman proposed a Special Theological Commission to study the spiritual state of the church.

Later in the summer of 1925, Bryan became the object of national attention during the Scopes trial, concerning the teaching of evolution in the public schools of Tennessee. Although Bryan won the case, public opinion turned against his militant style of defending a literally interpreted Bible, and the fundamentalist cause lost ground. In 1926, the Special Theological Commission issued an interim report affirming "the Christian principle of toleration." By 1927, the commission presented its final report. It argued that no one, not even the General Assembly, had the right to single out certain doctrines, such as the five points, and declare a particular interpretation of them to be "essential and necessary" for all. Only the judicial process of the church could determine points of doctrinal interpretation in specific cases. Fundamentalist control of the denomination was thus broken by shifting theological decision making to the presbyteries.

In 1929, the General Assembly approved a reorganization of the governing boards of Princeton Theological Seminary so that the exclusivist fundamentalists were no longer in control. Machen was outraged. With three other faculty members, he left to form Westminster Seminary in Philadelphia and, soon thereafter, the Independent Board for Presbyterian Foreign Missions, to counter what he felt was liberalism in the denomination's foreign mission program. The General Assembly declared this competition with a denominational agency unconstitutional and ordered all Presbyterians, including Machen, to desist from this activity. Machen refused, and in 1935 he left the denomination.

The year that Machen resigned from Princeton Seminary was, of course, the year of the stock market crash. During the 1930s, while Americans were reeling from the economic depression, the churches were suffering the consequences of the fundamentalist/modernist controversy. Machen and some of his most militant followers formed the Orthodox Presbyterian Church. Families, congregations, and denominations were divided as fundamentalists separated from mainline churches to form their own more homogeneous institutions.

By the late 1930s, most church people in America were tired of the tensions between the extremes on the left and right. Many wished to forget about theology, have peace, and get on with the practical work of the church. Into this vacuum came a new theological breeze blowing from Europe. It was not a well-defined school of thought but a new movement variously called "dialectical theology," "theology of crisis," "New Reformation theology," "neo-Calvinism," and "neo-orthodoxy." Among its most prominent figures were the Swiss theologians Barth and Brunner and the American Reinhold Niebuhr.

Neo-orthodoxy rejected the evolutionary idealism of liberalism, which had taught that human beings were basically good and that, by cooperating with God, people would bring the kingdom of God on earth. In contrast, Barth and others preached about human sin and a God of judgment and grace who would have to break into human history. At the same time, the neo-orthodox did not revert to the seventeenth-century orthodox assertion that God was revealed in the inerrant words of the Bible. The defining insight of early neo-orthodoxy was that God did not reveal information in an inspired book. God was revealed in the person of Jesus Christ. The Bible was a human, fallible, but unique and authoritative witness to the one revelation of God in Christ. A person's encounter with Christ in Scripture was the work of the Holy Spirit.

Most ministers in the mainline denominations in America welcomed neo-orthodoxy. During the 1940s and 1950s it made the Christian gospel freshly available and vital. After John A. Mackay became President of Princeton Seminary in 1936, that seminary became a center for the dissemination of this new model of doing theology. Neither Mackay nor others at Princeton wished to be doctrinaire Barthians, but they were grateful to Barth for the guiding insight that revelation came in Jesus Christ, to whom the Bible bears witness. This provided an alternative both to liberalism and to fundamentalism. Doctrinal affirmations could be drawn from Scripture without denying its literary flaws. By the late 1950s, neo-orthodoxy was well established as the working theological consensus in the Presbyterian Church. Barth and, through him, Calvin, rather than the propositions of the Westminster Confession, were the theological guides of Presbyterian theologians.

The Call for a Contemporary Confession

In 1956, the Presbytery of Amarillo (Texas) sent an overture to the General Assembly of the Presbyterian Church in the U.S.A. regarding the archaic language of the Westminster Shorter Catechism. The presbytery asked that the catechism be rewritten in contemporary language. The General Assembly responded by appointing a committee, chaired by Arthur Adams of Rochester, New York, to investigate the matter. In 1957, the Adams committee offered two alternatives. One was to prepare a historical introduction to the catechism and to revise the Scripture references attached to it. The other was that a committee be named to prepare "a brief statement of faith to be included in the Constitution after the union is consummated in 1958." The committee advocated the second option, stating that such an activity "should bring to all members of our Church some sense of participation in the thrilling revival of theology." The General Assembly chose the second option.

On May 28, 1958, the Presbyterian Church in the U.S.A. and the United Presbyterian Church of North America (UPNA) merged to form The United Presbyterian Church in the U.S.A. The confessional basis of the union was the Westminster standards, despite the fact that the UPNA had its own confession, written in 1925, which had superseded the Westminster Confession and its catechisms. Leaders in both denominations apparently anticipated confessional revision in the united church.

The uniting General Assembly in 1958 appointed nine men to the Special Committee on a Brief Contemporary Statement of Faith. Edward A. Dowey, Jr., a professor at Princeton Theological Seminary, was appointed chairman. During the next four years, eleven more members were added to the committee, including one laywoman. Of the original committee, one was unable to serve, two retired, and two others resigned.

After two meetings, the committee requested the General Assembly in 1959 for a broader mandate. Citing the need "to draw upon the fullness of our tradition and its origins in the Reformation period," the committee asked to study not only the Westminster standards but others, including the Heidelberg Catechism and the Second Helvetic Confession. By 1964, the final mandate of the committee, as approved by successive General Assemblies, was threefold:

> (1) fuller recognition of our own confessional history in the form of a book of creeds and confessions taken from the early, Reformation, and modern church; (2) a contemporary statement which is not a syllabus of all the topics of theology, but a confession of the meaning of Christ's reconciling work concretely in the life of the Church; and (3) the need, in the light of the first two points, for appropriate changes in the subscription formulas now in use for ministers, elders, and various other offices in the church.

The need for greater breadth of Reformed background was buttressed with heavy criticism of the Westminster standards. Their language and style were said to be generally unintelligible in the present. Furthermore, the Westminster Confession was equated with a seventeenth-century departure from the Reformation faith. Dowey asserted, "While Westminster is thus a post-Reformation statement, it is by no means a modern one. It derives from an age of scholastic theology, of preoccupation with authority and law, of churchly and political absolutism."

In 1965, the report of the Special Committee on a Brief Contemporary Statement of Faith was presented to the 177th General Assembly of The United Presbyterian Church in the U.S.A. The package consisted of a Book of Confessions, a revised statement of subscription for office-bearers in the denomination, and the contemporary Confession of 1967. The confession was structured around the theme of reconciliation. The preface stated:

> The Purpose of the Confession of 1967 is to call the church to that unity in confession and mission which is required of disciples today. This Confession is not a "system of doctrine," nor does it include all the traditional topics of theology. For example, the Trinity and

the Person of Christ are not redefined but are recognized and reaffirmed as forming the basis and determining the structure of the Christian faith.

God's reconciling work in Jesus Christ and the mission of reconciliation to which he has called his church are the heart of the gospel in any age. Our generation stands in peculiar need of reconciliation in Christ.

The confession was presented in three parts. First was "God's Work of Reconciliation," through Jesus Christ, through the Love of God, and through the Communion of the Holy Spirit. The role of the Bible was treated in a subsection on the Spirit. Second was "The Ministry of Reconciliation," divided into discussions of the Mission of the Church, which included reconciliation in society, and the Equipment of the Church, which included a discussion of preaching and teaching and the sacraments. Third was "The Fulfillment of Reconciliation" in the totality of human life in its environment and in the culmination of God's kingdom.

Controversy Over the Confession

Controversy over the proposed confession began months before it was presented to the General Assembly in 1965. Members of the committee who helped write it were interviewed, previews of the contents of the confession were given in public meetings, and magazine editors began praising, questioning, or condemning it, sometimes on the basis of incomplete information.

In May 1965, the General Assembly accepted the report of the Special Committee on a Brief Contemporary Statement of Faith by a wide margin. Procedures for discussing and eventually ratifying the new confession were established. A year for discussion of the confessional changes throughout the church with opportunity to offer amendments was declared. The Moderator, William P. Thompson, appointed a Special Committee of Fifteen, including ministers and elders, to receive and consider proposed amendments.

The Special Committee of Fifteen, chaired by the Rev. W. Sherman Skinner, held seven two- to three-day meetings. Correspondence addressed to the committee numbered nearly 1,100 letters, often lengthy ones. Many people accepted a general invitation to appear before the committee in person to present their views.

Responses to the proposed confessional revisions were channeled in part through two new organizations which came into being at that time. Presbyterians United for Biblical Confession, or PUBC, was composed primarily of conservative ministers and theologians. Its stated purpose was to propose revisions to the Confession of 1967 which would make it, in PUBC's view, more biblical in content and evangelical in orientation. The chairman of the group, the Rev. Dr. Cary Weisiger III, stressed that members of PUBC had no intention of being divisive and were dedicated to working through appropriate channels to achieve their ends. PUBC sponsored public meetings to discuss the new confession and published articles that questioned elements of it. The principal desires for revision developed by PUBC were five:

> (1) A paragraph on the deity of Christ as emphatic as the one proposed on his humanity; (2) a statement on the inspiration and unique authority of the Scriptures; (3) a statement on the utter necessity of individual response in repentance and faith under the power of the Holy Spirit to complete God's purpose of reconciliation in Jesus Christ; (4) an application of the moral law as expounded by Jesus Christ to matters of social concern such as the "new morality," divorce, drunkenness, and delinquency; (5) the strengthening of the subscription questions to give true confessional status and power to the confessions of the church.

Another organization, formed somewhat earlier, was the Presbyterian Lay Committee, Inc. Its members were predominantly laypeople, many of whom were highly placed executives in American corporations. In its statement of purpose, the Lay Committee announced:

> The last fifty years have witnessed a growing effort within the Church to act as a corporate body in efforts to influence government and people in economic, social, and political affairs instead of first converting men to Christianity and then encouraging those men to fill their individual role as Christians in civic affairs. . . . The mission of the Church is to call all men to redemption, and only as she redeems individual people will society be effectively transformed.

At first, the Lay Committee was reluctant to become involved in doctrinal issues. Then it became apparent that the Confession of 1967's stance on reconciliation in society provided theological sanction for the church's recent corporate stands on race, war, poverty, and other social concerns. An article in *The New York Times* reported that the Confession of 1967 would be the "first theological statement from the Reformed or Calvinistic branch of Protestantism to discuss social ethics and support church participation in social issues." On the other side, *Christianity Today* editorialized that the silence of former confessions signified that the church should not involve itself in social issues and that the new confession would "legitimize contemporary church practices which violate the Westminster Standards." In the end, the Lay Committee officially opposed the Confession of 1967.

When the General Assembly met in Boston in 1966, it had not only to deal with revisions in the draft version of the Confession of 1967 but to elect a new Stated Clerk. Eugene Carson Blake, after many years in the post, was leaving to become the new General Secretary of the World Council of Churches. In an upset, the retiring Moderator, attorney William P. Thompson, was nominated from the floor and elected over a clergyman who was the "unanimous recommendation" of the nominating committee. Thompson was known to share Blake's ecumenical vision and concern for civil rights but was viewed as more tactful and less domineering than Blake and less likely to be involved in overt acts of civil disobedience. Thompson had, however, strongly supported the proposed Confession of 1967 and had worked hard during his moderatorial year to calm fears and gather suggestions for the revision committee.

A revised version of the Confession of 1967 was presented to the Assembly by the Special Committee of Fifteen. Chairman Skinner noted nine areas of concern in which revisions and additions had been made. The four substantial concerns of PUBC, for example, had been incorporated; only their suggestions regarding subscription of church officers had not been heeded. Even an additional item on personal morality had been added in response to conservative concern, a paragraph on "anarchy in sexual relationships" with an affirmation of the value of faithful, loving marriage and parenthood. Leaders of PUBC declared themselves satisfied with the result and pledged to work for passage of the revised confession.

The modified version of the Confession of 1967 was passed by the Assembly on a voice vote. It was then submitted to the one hundred and eighty-eight presbyteries for their discussion and decision. Interest was high. Over 130,000 copies of a booklet, *Report of the Special Committee on a Brief Contemporary Statement of Faith to The United Presbyterian Church in the United States of America, May, 1965,* were sold. During the several months of debate in the presbyteries, two unresolved issues occupied most of the attention. Public attention was focused by the active opposition of the Lay Committee to these two items. Just after Christmas 1966, the Lay Committee took out full-page advertisements in 100 major newspapers around the country. They urged Presbyterians to vote against the Confession of 1967 in their presbyteries because of its statements on the nature of the Bible and because of the church's attitude toward international conflict.

The Place of the Bible

The final statement on the Bible in the Confession of 1967 represented a careful political compromise between the original drafting committee, which wished to reserve the designation "Word of God" for Jesus Christ alone, and those who believed that it properly applied to Scripture as well. The original form of the Confession of 1967 stated, "The one sufficient revelation of God is Jesus Christ, the Word of God incarnate, to whom the Holy Spirit bears witness in many ways." The Bible was described as "the normative witness to this revelation." The revised statement read, "The one sufficient revelation of God is Jesus Christ, the Word of God incarnate, to whom the Holy Spirit bears unique and authoritative witness throughout the Holy Scriptures, which are received and obeyed as the word of God written." The distinction favored by the drafting committee was retained by the use of a capital "W" to designate Christ as the Word of God and a small "w" in reference to Scripture.

PUBC supported the revised version of the Confession of 1967 regarding the Bible, as did most denominational leaders. One of the principal authors of the original draft, George Hendry of Princeton Seminary, appeared angered by it. In the October 1966 issue of the *Princeton Seminary Bulletin,* Hendry referred to the revised document as a "hodgepodge which attempts to combine the viewpoints of 1967 and 1647." He objected especially to language about the Bible as a "rule of faith" when the original intention of the drafting committee had been to represent the Bible only as a "means of grace." "Division in the Church has been avoided at the cost of an unstable theological compromise," Hendry warned.

The Lay Committee, however, felt that the changes had not gone far enough. In its newspaper ads, the Lay Committee alleged:

> How far the authors would go in humanizing the Bible can be realized in this excerpt from the new Confession: "The Scriptures, given under the guidance of the Holy Spirit, are nevertheless the words of men, conditioned by the language, thought forms, and literary fashions of the places and times at which they were written."

Such a statement was one reason to vote against the proposed confession, the Lay Committee urged.

The Risk of National Security

The other very sore point for the Lay Committee and many others was located in statements in the Confession of 1967 regarding war. In a section on "Reconciliation in Society," the Confession declared:

> God's reconciliation in Jesus Christ is the ground of the peace, justice, and freedom among nations which all powers of government are called to serve and defend. The church, in its own life, is called to practice the forgiveness of enemies and to commend to the nations as practical politics the search for cooperation and peace. This search requires that the nations pursue fresh and responsible relations across every line of conflict, even at risk to national security, to reduce areas of strife and to broaden international understanding. Reconciliation among nations becomes peculiarly urgent as countries develop nuclear, chemical, and biological weapons, diverting their manpower and resources from constructive uses and risking the annihilation of mankind. Although nations may serve God's purposes in history, the church

which identifies the sovereignty of any one nation or any one way of life with the cause of God denies the Lordship of Christ and betrays its calling.

The Presbytery of Washington, D.C., protested that the phrase "even at risk to national security" was "unnecessarily provocative." An overture to the 1967 General Assembly was prepared asking, as soon as the Confession of 1967 was adopted, that it immediately be amended to remove this phrase. Many elders in that presbytery worked in the Pentagon. Secretary of Defense Robert McNamara, a Presbyterian elder, had already publicly expressed his concern over the implications of the "disarmament mentality" suggested by the Confession. The Lay Committee argued that such language represented an unwarranted intrusion by the church into matters beyond its sphere of competence.

The Conclusion of the Matter

The issues had been so complex and emotions had run so high, Dowey thought. Yet substantially more than the required two thirds of the presbyteries had voted approval of the confessional change. The more important issue was whether the church would actually be guided by its new *Book of Confessions* or whether it would just put the volume on a shelf. But now the immediate problem remained. Would the Committee on Bills and Overtures uphold the constitutionality of the process of confessional revision? Or would they vote to block the Confession of 1967 and the *Book of Confessions* on a technicality? As he looked at the committee, Dowey mused: nine years of work—would they be for nothing?

The Bills and Overtures Committee of the 1967 General Assembly approved the constitutionality of the process of confessional revision by a vote of 19 for and 3 against, and one abstention. The three members who voted negatively presented a minority report. After hearing the arguments, the Assembly voted about 4 to 1 to approve the proposal to revise the confessional position of The United Presbyterian Church in the U.S.A.

Ecumenical concern was expressed by Professor Arthur C. Cochrane of Dubuque Theological Seminary. He proposed, and the Assembly adopted, a statement that "this 179th General Assembly humbly commend this our Confession of 1967 to other Christian churches—Roman Catholic, Orthodox, and Protestant—for their prayerful consideration and study, that if need be, this our confession, may be corrected out of God's mouth, the Holy Scriptures; and that this our confession of reconciliation in Christ, or some such confession, may be the confession of the one, holy catholic church of Jesus Christ in this land."

The Bills and Overtures Committee, by the narrow margin of 12 to 11, also recommended that the Assembly take no action on the overture from the Presbytery of Washington, D.C., recommending immediate amendment of the new confession to delete the phrase "even at risk to national security." The air had been cleared somewhat by a statement of the Department of Defense that it felt the Confession of 1967 would not prevent Presbyterians from serving their country in any capacity whatsoever. After significant discussion, the Assembly sustained the recommendation. The Confession of 1967 remained in the form adopted by the presbyteries and affirmed by the General Assembly of 1967. It was thus available to guide the church in facing the social upheavals of the late 1960s and 1970s.

Essential Tenets of the Reformed Faith

Reconciliation

"God's reconciling work in Jesus Christ and the mission of reconciliation to which he has called his church are the heart of the gospel in any age. Our generation stands in peculiar need of reconciliation in Christ. Accordingly this Confession of 1967 is built upon that theme." Thus ends the Preface to the Confession of 1967, giving the rationale and setting the scene for what is to follow. Reconciliation is at the heart of the Christian message, and it was what Americans most needed to hear in the mid-sixties.

Edward A. Dowey, Jr., chair of the committee which drafted the Confession of 1967, gave valuable insight into the thinking of the committee in his book *A Commentary on the Confession of 1967 and an Introduction to "The Book of Confessions,"* published by The Westminster Press in 1968. In principle, the Confession of 1967 did not quote biblical passages, except in the concluding ascription of praise. The biblical passage from which the theme of reconciliation was drawn, however, was 2 Corinthians 5:19, "God was in Christ reconciling the world to himself." Calvin called this "the best passage of all" on justification by faith. Dowey linked that Pauline passage with the familiar words of Jesus in Matthew 5:24, "first be reconciled to your brother, and then come and offer your gift" (at the altar). These passages manifest the two movements in reconciliation: God comes to humanity in forgiveness, and people are to be peacemakers with their fellow human beings.

For Dowey, the biblical covenant was the "hidden agenda" within the structure of the Confession of 1967. The three motifs of "God's Work of Reconciliation," "The Ministry of Reconciliation," and "The Fulfillment of Reconciliation," were a contemporary way of manifesting three dimensions of the covenant theme: the grace of God which called together a people to serve, the service to which they are called, and the promise which causes people to continue in hope and not to despair.

The reconciliation proclaimed in Scripture is, in the first instance, one-sided. God acts to reconcile the world to himself. Secondly, reconciliation presupposes conflict. If there were no problems, if people were not at cross-purposes, reconciliation would not be needed. The seriousness of the need for reconciliation and God's determination to bring it about are demonstrated by Christ's death on the cross. It is through the presence of the Spirit of Christ in human life that we are empowered to act in reconciling ways toward other people. Finally, reconciliation in human affairs always remains a promise, never a fully realized accomplishment. It is an ultimate truth which enables us to continue to move forward to God's promised consummation in perfect justice and love.

The Equality of Persons

The Confession of 1967 broke new ground in Reformed confessional history by explicitly addressing four contemporary social problems: racial discrimination, peace among nations, enslaving poverty in a world of abundance, and relationships between women and men. A Christian response to these problems is based in the biblical understanding that all people are equal in God's sight. "There is neither Jew nor Greek, there is neither slave nor free, there is neither male nor female; for you are all one in Christ Jesus" (Gal. 3:28). In its concrete application of the reconciliation motif to specific social and ethical problems, the Confession of 1967 went beyond the resources available in Barth and neo-orthodoxy. It opened Presbyterians to new insights which the theology of liberation would present in the 1970s.

The writers of the Confession of 1967 had prophetic insight in the biblical sense of prophecy: speaking a word from God into a contemporary situation. How each of these problems would enlarge in the late 1960s and the 1970s, the members of the committee could not have known. The civil rights struggle became more critical and confused with the assassination of Martin Luther King, Jr., in 1968. The war in Vietnam increased in its violence, and public reaction to it expanded in vigor. Americans began to be aware of the economic inequities between the European and North American world and the Third World of Latin America, Africa, Asia, and the Pacific basin. Only in the 1970s did Americans begin to focus on the issue of the equality of women and men. The church was sensitized to sexism in language and practice, especially as women began to take a larger role in the leadership of governing bodies and to attend seminary in larger numbers in preparation for the ministry. Each of these issues emphasized that the biblical motif of reconciliation, in practical terms, required awareness and application of the reality that from the viewpoint of Christian faith all people are equal.

Contemporary Relevance

Racial Discrimination

Racial discrimination has not ceased in the United States. Despite all the progress made in recent years, blacks, and especially black women, fall at the bottom of the charts on economic progress. In the realm of social acceptance, discrimination has taken new and more subtle forms. Now we are becoming aware of the barriers to equal status facing other racial minorities, especially Hispanics and the various peoples who have come from Asia. The statements in the Confession of 1967 continue to have relevance. The Presbyterian Church (U.S.A.) continues to advocate racial equality and to implement affirmative action in its own practices.

The lead taken by the Confession of 1967 in making racial discrimination a confessional issue was followed by the World Alliance of Reformed Churches (WARC) at its 21st General Council meeting at Ottawa, Canada, in August 1982. WARC is an association for communication and cooperation among 157 member churches worldwide with a total membership of some 80 million people. These churches represent the larger Reformed family tree of which the Presbyterian Church (U.S.A.) is one branch.

The General Council meets infrequently, the previous gathering having been in Nairobi, Kenya, in 1970. Thus much important business needed to be done.

Two all-white Dutch Reformed churches of South Africa (the Nederduitse Gereformeerde Kerk and the Nederduitse Hervormde Kerk), members of the World Alliance of Reformed Churches, had persistently endorsed and defended their government's policy of apartheid, or racial separation, which they preferred to call "separate development." For more than twenty years, other Reformed churches within WARC, and the association itself, had carried on serious discussions about this matter with the South Africans. No change in their stance had occurred. Indeed, the white South African Reformed churches had broken ties with their mother church in the Netherlands and had withdrawn from membership in the World Council of Churches over this issue.

At the General Council of WARC in Ottawa, two notable actions were taken to accent the unacceptability of racial discrimination. First, the Rev. Dr. Allan Boesak, Chaplain at the University of the Western Cape and a minister of the Dutch Reformed Mission Church (Coloured)—who would be preacher to the General Assembly of the Presbyterian Church (U.S.A.) in 1984—was elected president of WARC. Second, the Alliance "reluctantly and painfully" acted to suspend from membership the two all-white Dutch Reformed denominations. The rationale was that racial discrimination is a *status confessionis,* an issue of confessional status.

The General Council declared "that apartheid ('Separate Development') is a *sin* and that *the moral and theological justification of it* is a travesty of the gospel and, in its persistent disobedience to the Word of God, a theological heresy." But apartheid is not a heresy. Heresy is a distortion of Christian truth, and there is nothing Christian about apartheid. It is simply a sin. The heresy is the attempt to justify a policy of systematic racial discrimination on moral and theological grounds. To do this is to pervert the Christian doctrines of God, creation, and humanity. The General Council expressed hope that it would be possible to restore the suspended members to fellowship. And it confessed its own guilt and complicity in racism.

Peace Among Nations

The reuniting General Assembly of the Presbyterian Church (U.S.A.) proclaimed the 1980s a Decade of Peacemaking. The theological justification for this emphasis was grounded in God's covenant of grace with creation. Peace was understood as *shalom,* the biblical concept of the wholeness in which individuals and the human community are meant to live. God's peace heals, comforts, strengthens, and frees. Only in God's covenant can the church and the world experience wholeness, security, and justice.

Congregations were encouraged to incorporate peacemaking as a central part of their life and mission. A seven-point program was suggested, beginning with (1) worship; (2) receiving God's peace through Bible study and prayer; and (3) growth as peacemakers in family life, congregation, and community. It continued by encouraging each congregation to (4) act for social, racial, and economic justice for those in the local community; (5) support human rights and economic justice efforts in at least one area of the world; (6) work to end the arms race, reverse the worldwide growth of militarism, and reduce tension among nations; and (7) support financially the church-wide peacemaking effort.

The theological rationale and the seven-point program make clear that peacemaking is a comprehensive concept for contemporary Presbyterians. The part of that emphasis which has perhaps received the most attention is the concern to halt the nuclear arms race. This is not a new departure for Presbyterians. General Assembly statements for the past three decades, beginning in 1956, have called attention to the dangers of the proliferation of weapons of mass destruction. In 1980 and 1981, the predecessor denominations of the Presbyterian Church (U.S.A.) adopted the report "Peacemaking: The Believers' Calling" and designated peacemaking as a priority. In 1981 and 1982 those same denominations endorsed a "Call to Halt the Nuclear Arms Race," which said:

> To improve national and international security, the United States and the Soviet Union should stop the nuclear arms race. Specifically, they should adopt a mutual freeze on the testing, production, and deployment of nuclear weapons and of missiles and new aircraft designed primarily to deliver nuclear weapons. This is an essential, verifiable first step toward lessening the risk of nuclear war and reducing the nuclear arsenals.

The directions which the Confession of 1967 indicated in the arena of peace among nations continue to be followed by the Presbyterian Church (U.S.A.).

An arresting parallel is found in an action of the Reformed Alliance of Churches in the Federal Republic of Germany. In 1982, they brought to the General Council of the World Alliance of Reformed Churches a "Confession of Faith in Jesus Christ and the Responsibility of the Church for Peace." They noted, significantly, "As Germans we are living in the focal point of the tensions between the two great military power-blocks, in a zone with the greatest concentration of atomic weapons anywhere in the world, both launch pad and target of a conceivable 'limited atomic war' which could extend into a universal holocaust." With this background, they stated:

> Now, as the possibility of atomic war is more than ever before becoming a probability, we come to this recognition: The issue of peace is a confessional issue. For us the *status confessionis* is given with it because the attitude taken to means of mass destruction has to do with the affirmation or denial of the Gospel itself.

Enslaving Poverty

According to news reports in 1983, the world spends $1.3 million every minute for military purposes. Every minute, thirty children die for want of food and medicines. The issues of peacemaking and economic justice are thus not unrelated. The cost of one new nuclear submarine equals the annual education budget of 23 developing countries with 160 million school-age children. It is difficult to react emotionally to statistics. Yet the figures are staggering: a current world military budget of $660 billion per year; a stockpile of 50,000 nuclear weapons; 25 million soldiers under arms; 1 billion people living under military-controlled governments; and more than 9 million civilians killed in "conventional" wars since Hiroshima. Military spending has an enormous human cost.

In 1984, the 196th General Assembly of the Presbyterian Church (U.S.A) approved for study by the churches a lengthy paper entitled "Christian Faith and Economic Justice." This was the result of a study authorized in 1978 by the former Presbyterian Church in the U.S. and assigned to its Council on Theology and Culture. It utilized the expertise of persons trained both in theology and economics.

The paper begins with an extended treatment of the biblical materials relating to economic justice and the theological implications of those biblical statements. The Reformed concepts of the covenant, the sovereignty of God, human sin, and our responsibility as stewards of God's creation provide a foundation for reflection leading to six demands of justice which are implied in the biblical and theological study. The paper goes on to describe the global economic situation in which God calls us to faithfulness. A detailed analysis of both capitalism and socialism as economic systems is provided. The paper then concludes with a final chapter in which the question is asked: "What does faithfulness to God require?"

So serious and extensive a study shows that the church still takes seriously the assertion of the Confession of 1967 that "enslaving poverty in a world of abundance is an intolerable violation of God's good creation." Presbyterians have disagreed and will continue to disagree about the appropriate public policy actions to combat unjust and immoral conditions. Debate about the means of action is both legitimate and potentially helpful. But Presbyterians need both to study and to agree on the biblical and theological principles by which they are to operate. This book and such study documents as the one just mentioned are designed as means to that necessary end.

The Equality of Women and Men

Presbyterians have been struggling to act out the full equality of women and men all during the twentieth century. Women were ordained as deacons as early as 1906 in the former United Presbyterian Church of North America. The first attempt to ordain a woman as a minister in the former United Presbyterian Church in the U.S.A., and its predecessor denominations, was made in 1911. The Presbytery of Chemung in New York voted to take a woman theology student under its care, but the General Assembly ruled that it was inexpedient. In 1929, overtures were sent to the General Assembly asking the ordination of women as ministers, ruling elders, and local evangelists. Only the overture on the ordination of women as ruling elders was declared passed in 1930. For the next several decades, the emphasis was on commissioned lay workers who did religious education. These were primarily women. In 1955 there were 221 women in these positions and only 16 men.

By the 1950s, approximately 80 percent of all Protestant denominations ordained women in some capacity. In 1953, the Presbytery of Rochester sent an overture to the General Assembly to "initiate actions necessary to permit the ordination of women to the ministry of Jesus Christ." The

General Assembly appointed a special committee to study the subject. It reported in 1955, proposing an overture to be sent to the presbyteries, stating, "Both men and women may be called to this office." In 1956, the General Assembly ratified what had by then been approved by the presbyteries. Women now had the right to be ordained both as ruling elders and as ministers.

A struggle over the implementation of this permission for women to be ordained characterized the 1970s. In the mid-1970s the former UPCUSA was preoccupied with what was known as the Kenyon case. A young Pittsburgh Theological Seminary graduate, Walter Wynn Kenyon, announced to the Candidates and Credentials Committee of Pittsburgh Presbytery that in conscience he could not participate in the ordination of women to the ministry because he believed that the Bible forbade it. The committee recommended against his ordination, but the Presbytery of Pittsburgh overruled its committee and voted to ordain Kenyon. A judicial case resulted. In 1974, the Permanent Judicial Commission (PJC) of The United Presbyterian Church in the U.S.A. overruled the presbytery and declared that Kenyon could not be ordained.

The decision of the Permanent Judicial Commission in the Kenyon case appealed to the Confession of 1967 for theological justification of its act:

> Presbytery's power is not absolute. It must be exercised in conformity with the Constitution. In other words, our polity is a government of law rather than of men. . . . The question of the importance of our belief in the equality of all people before God is thus essential to the disposition in this case. . . . It is evident from our Church's confessional standards that the Church believes the Spirit of God has led us into new understandings of this equality before God. Thus the Confession of 1967 proclaims, "Congregations, individuals, or groups of Christians who exclude, dominate, or patronize their fel-

lowmen, however subtly, resist the Spirit of God and bring contempt on the faith which they profess" (C.9.44). The UPCUSA, in obedience to Jesus Christ, under the authority of Scripture (and guided by its confessions) has now developed its understanding of the equality of all people (both male and female) before God. It has expressed this understanding in the Book of Order with such clarity as to make the candidate's stated position a rejection of its government and discipline.

There is both irony and encouragement in the decision of the PJC, which cited the Confession of 1967 to justify its commitment to the equality of all persons. The irony is that the Confession of 1967 did not directly address the need to correct the remaining inequalities between women and men in the church. Theologians and church persons generally did not become sensitive to that issue until a few years later. We were especially insensitive to the power of patriarchal language in perpetuating these inequalities. In 1967, male-oriented language was commonly and uncritically accepted. The Confession of 1967 routinely says "men" when it refers to people, both women and men. The first study of sexist language in the Presbyterian Church was not initiated until 1973 and was only received, not adopted, by the Church when presented in 1975. Further studies have been done and have had useful effect. In 1982, in connection with a symposium at Princeton Seminary on "The Confession of 1967: Contemporary Implications," two women, the Rev. Cynthia A. Jarvis and Prof. Freda A. Gardner, prepared an inclusive-language text of the Confession of 1967 which has been used unofficially.

The encouragement is that we can learn and change. Every confession is helpful to the extent that it clearly addresses issues current in its own time and culture. Insofar as it is relevant to one time period, it also runs the risk of being dated and not as directly relevant at a later time. That should not be cause for dismay. It only means that we must continue to be a confessing church. We must return to the Scriptures in every generation to find direction and guidance for the problems that are current.

In the words of the pastor of our Pilgrim forebears, John Robinson, "God has yet more light to break forth from his Word." The earlier confessions did not explicitly draw the conclusion from Scripture that women and men are equal. The practice of their culture obscured their vision of this biblical truth, just as for so long the equality of people of all races was not understood and practiced. But now, changes in our world have forced us to look again at Scripture and understand more clearly the liberating direction in which it points. The pattern of bringing our new problems to Scripture is one we should follow in each generation.

In Presbyterianism, our polity should always be founded on biblically and confessionally grounded theology. We must remember that, in a Reformed context, "more light" always comes from God's Word in Scripture. We do not rely on a subjective Quaker inner light. We are always obligated to study and reflect, as well as to pray and feel, in coming to our decisions. But we can learn something new. Our present blinders can gradually be peeled away. As we listen to one another in the Christian community, we can discover the limitations of our own perspectives. Helping one another, we need to bring each new issue to Scripture, Calvin's "spectacles" that can give us clearer vision. The process of writing a new confession in the 1980s may be the occasion for us both to reaffirm what we have learned from the past and to launch out into fresh insights from God's Word.

11

Faith and Practice

"There is an inseparable connection between faith and practice." Those words have a contemporary ring. They accord well with our modern attitude, which judges beliefs pragmatically, by whether they really make a difference. But those words are not new. They are as old as Presbyterianism in America. They come from the "Historic Principles of Church Order" drawn up in 1788 by the Synod of New York and Philadelphia and adopted the following year as part of the general plan of government by the first General Assembly of the Presbyterian Church in the United States of America. The whole paragraph is worth repeating and reflecting on:

> That truth is in order to goodness; and the great touchstone of truth, its tendency to promote holiness, according to our Savior's rule, "By their fruits ye shall know them." And that no opinion can be either more pernicious or more absurd than that which brings truth and falsehood upon a level, and represents it as of no consequence what a man's opinions are. On the contrary, we are persuaded that there is an inseparable connection between faith and practice, truth and duty. Otherwise, it would be of no consequence either to discover the truth or to embrace it.
>
> (*The Book of Order,* G-1.0304)

The reason for studying doctrines, for reflecting on what is essential in the Reformed faith, is that we might bear fruit, do better, live according to God's will in this world. Theology is a practical discipline.

Theology as Reflection

The contemporary Dutch Reformed theologian Gerrit C. Berkouwer once said, "Theology is scientific reflection on the normativity of revelation for faith." That is a mouthful. But its elements are instructive. Theology in one sense is something that everyone does. We all have some sort of faith; we have beliefs and commitments that guide our lives. We usually don't know where we got them, and we certainly couldn't prove that they were true. Christian faith, however, is directed toward and based upon the revelation of God in Jesus Christ which is recorded in Scripture. The revelation is "normative" for us. "Norm" originally meant an absolute standard. In a class, the norm is an "A" grade. Now we have accepted the notion that what most people do is the norm, so we equate norm with average. The average grade may be a "C." The revelation of God is not something that we can take lightly. It is the norm in the original sense: the standard of our lives. All people are theologians in this sense. We all begin in faith and follow some sort of standard. Christians try to follow the standard of the Word of God.

How well we act on the rest of Berkouwer's definition determines whether we will be good-to-excellent theologians or fair-to-poor ones. Theology involves "reflection." We ought to think about the implications of what Scripture says. That is what doctrines are, attempts to summarize and generalize the lessons learned from a lot of comparing Scripture with Scripture. Really good theology also demands "scientific" reflection. The word "scientific" in Berkouwer's Continental European sense does not mean what we usually take it to be. It does not mean natural science or technology. It just means the careful disciplined study of something. You could approach politics or music or sports scientifically. That would indicate you accepted the discipline of learning about a particular field of human activity and would use the best information and the best approaches available to study it.

By reading this book you have moved forward as a theologian. You have done some study and reflection on the doctrines that are central to the revelation of God in Jesus Christ to which Scripture bears witness. Now you are ready to do more. This book is a guide to studying the confessions themselves, not a substitute for doing so. And the confessions are meant to be used as a guide in our own direct, personal study of the Bible.

The Book of Order calls the central biblical doctrines we have examined "essential tenets of the Reformed faith." The sixteen doctrines we have studied are not all one needs to know from Scripture and the confessions. They include, however, the ten doctrines mentioned in Chapter II of *The Book of Order* and, taken together, they give us an idea of what it means to be catholic—ecumenically Christian—Protestant, and Reformed.

The creeds and confessions and theological declarations in our Presbyterian *Book of Confessions* represent the theological reflections of centuries of Christians who have preceded us. It is remarkable what a unified testimony these documents offer, when we consider the differences in time and place and cultural context of their development. Each confession has its own peculiarities, of course. Sometimes there are statements we simply do not accept today, such as that the pope is the anti-Christ. But we accept the confessions, not in the sense that we are bound by every word but in the attitude that we will be guided by the central affirmations they share. These central affirmations are what *The Book of Order* calls the "essential tenets," or beliefs, of the confessions.

Office-bearers in the Presbyterian Church (U.S.A.) say that they will "sincerely receive and adopt" these essential tenets of the Reformed faith "as expressed in the confessions of our church." Why? Because we believe that they are "authentic and reliable expressions of what Scripture leads us to believe and do." Thus ministers, elders, and deacons vow to "be instructed and led" by those confessions as they "lead the people of God." What is necessary for the leaders is surely helpful for all church members. And they could be instructive for inquirers into the meaning of the Christian faith in its Reformed expression. If you are a minister, an elder, or a deacon, by studying the essential tenets of *The Book of Confessions* you put vitality into the vow you took at your ordination. Now you can work at the application of these doctrinal truths. "Truth is in order to goodness"; there is a connection between faith and practice.

Theology is not something that someone else can do for you. Nor is theology ever done once and for all. The confessions are guides for us in the task of doing our own reflection on the Word of God in our generation. We should not act as if we are the first people ever to think about these things. The great value of the confessions is that they enable us to build on the wisdom of the past. But neither can we rest on the past. The Christian faith, the Reformed faith, must be reunderstood and reasserted in every generation. The process of preparing a new brief statement of the Reformed faith in the 1980s can be the occasion for reappropriating our biblical and Reformed heritage in this generation. The whole church needs to be involved, because the process is at least as instructive as the final product. This book is meant as an encouragement for all persons in the Presbyterian Church (U.S.A.) to be involved in reflecting on our confessional past in order to be better able to say and do something relevant in the present.

Theology as Dialogue

Doing theology means being in a continual dialogue. The first and essential dialogue is with the Word of God, the living Word, Jesus Christ, found in the written Word, Scripture. Reflecting on the Presbyterian creeds is a second necessary dialogue with the Christian tradition, especially in its Reformed expression. We need also to carry on a dialogue within the Christian community. We Presbyterians need to talk to each other. And we need to hear other Christian voices which complement and challenge our own. The case studies on the historical context of the confessions have shown our Reformed ancestors often in angry disagreement with Roman Catholics, Lutherans, and Anabaptists. None of those groups are precisely where they were when the past confessions were written. Nor are we. Great strides have been made in coming to common understandings with Roman Catholics, where once there seemed to be chasms which could not be bridged, especially since the Second Vatican Council in the 1960s. The Lutheran-Reformed dialogues of recent years have evidenced remarkable unanimity of mind and heart despite past differences in expression. And we have a much greater appreciation for the values of the Anabaptist tradition and have been reminded not to judge any group by only its most extreme examples.

There is not only the dialogue that goes on within the church. We need also to be in continual dialogue with the world. Human experience can help us to understand more of God's Word and will for our lives. Calvin began his *Institutes of the Christian Religion* with the observation, "Nearly all the wisdom we possess, that is to say, true and sound wisdom, consists of two parts: the knowledge of God and of ourselves. But, while joined by many bonds, which one precedes and brings forth the other is not easy to discern." We can learn from all of life. We need to be in dialogue with every dimension of our culture. Especially we need to learn from new discoveries in the sciences: physical, biological, and social. We can always learn from the arts. And every movement for human betterment can sensitize us to listen more carefully to God's concerns for all people, especially those who have few human advocates.

The sections about contemporary relevance in this book are meant to stimulate that dialogue, within the church and with the world. Whether one agrees or disagrees with a particular application of Reformed doctrine is not so important as that one is actively involved in the dialogue between the Reformed faith and our contemporary culture.

It is most important to realize that there are concentric circles of authority. In our Presbyterian ordination vows, we move from the center outward as we are asked to minister "in obedience to Jesus Christ, under the authority of Scripture, and continually guided by our confessions." That is an appropriate descending order of importance. It is yet one further level away from the center when we apply a confessional statement to some particular program or policy. We need to stay open and in dialogue with one another about the appropriateness of our applications of doctrine even when we feel most deeply about them. There is often more than one way that a particular biblical and confessional truth can be applied. We must all live in the strength of our convictions. But we are unwise to try to coerce others to comply with particular applications of our convictions, especially in the area of public policy. "God alone is Lord of the conscience" is the first of the Historic Principles of Church Order.

Calvin as a Reformed Theologian

The Reformed tradition is often referred to as Calvinism. One of the ironies of our present *Book of Confessions* is that we have no confession written by Calvin and thus, in this book, no case study of Calvin, either of his historical context or of his contribution. Those who compiled the present *Book of Confessions* were certainly not hostile to Calvin. Among them were outstanding students of Calvin's life and thought. It may be that they were so steeped in Calvin that they were consciously trying to add other important influences from the Reformation period. Certainly we are indebted to them for the richness which has resulted.

The Proposed Book of Confessions, which was considered by the Presbyterian Church in the United States in 1976 but never adopted, included the Geneva Catechism prepared by Calvin and published in 1541. Calvin said, "the Church of God will never preserve itself without a Catechism, for it is like the seed to keep the good grain from dying out, and causing it to multiply from age to age." Calvin believed that the church would not be truly reformed unless its children were continually instructed in the essentials of the Christian religion. The Geneva Catechism fulfilled that function by providing a simple and straightforward exposition of the Christian faith through discussion of the Apostles' Creed, the Ten Commandments, the Lord's Prayer, and the sacraments of Baptism and the Lord's Supper.

Why has Calvin been so important to the Presbyterian tradition? Perhaps it is because he embodied so many of those qualities which Christians, and especially Presbyterians, prize. We need look at only three as illustrations.

Calvin as Educator

Presbyterians esteem education and John Calvin was a superb scholar. He was born in 1509 in Noyon, France. His father, an accountant for the local cathedral and a devout Roman Catholic, sent him to school to become a priest. Calvin studied languages and philosophy and received his master's degree in theology at the age of eighteen. His father, after a dispute at the cathedral, redirected his son toward the more lucrative profession of law. John complied and received a doctorate in law at Orleans in 1532. Immediately he left for Paris to study literature, especially Hebrew and Greek, at the university there.

The University of Paris was by then in the throes of response to the Protestant Reformation. Calvin experienced what he described as a "sudden conversion." He resigned his church scholarship and fled to Switzerland. In the following months, many of his friends were arrested and burned at the stake in France. Calvin felt that they were faithful servants of God and resolved not to remain silent. At the age of twenty-seven, he published his *Institutes of the Christian Religion.* (The word translated as "institutes" simply meant "instruction" or "education.") Calvin intended it to show the Christian faith in its simplicity and clarity. He added a Prefatory Address to the King of France in hopes of gaining support for the Protestant cause.

Calvin's *Institutes,* modeled on the Apostles' Creed, went through numerous editions between the first in 1536 and the last in 1559, growing into a textbook of theology which was formative for the whole of Reformed Protestantism. It has been called the supreme theological structure of the Protestant Reformation and would occupy a place on any short list of books which have notably affected the course of history. Calvin's scholarship further unfolded in volumes of tracts and essays and in commentaries on nearly every book of the Bible. About 4,000 letters remain from his extensive correspondence with other church leaders of the day. As Luther was the prophet of Protestantism, so Calvin was its educator.

Calvin as Administrator

In August 1536, Calvin was traveling to Strasbourg when he was forced to detour through Geneva to avoid the clash of German and French armies. He stopped at an inn and registered under an assumed name. But he was recognized by another Frenchman, William Farel. This Farel had spearheaded the Reformation in Geneva, persuading the town council to suspend the Mass. But he needed help, and Calvin seemed the answer to his prayers. As Calvin reports it:

> Farel, burning with wondrous zeal, suddenly set all his efforts at keeping me. After having heard that I was determined to pursue my own private studies—when Farel realized he could get nowhere by pleas—he came to the point of a curse: that it would please God to curse my leisure and the quiet for my studies that I sought, if in such grave emergency I should withdraw and refuse to give help. This so overwhelmed me that I desisted from my journey.

Against his will, then, Calvin became the leader of the Reformation in Geneva. He preached, taught, and prepared a Confession of Faith, a Book of Discipline, and a Catechism for the church. He organized the public school system and worked with the town council on plans for a "model city."

Inevitably, the changes initiated by Calvin and Farel went too far for some influential citizens. In January 1538 they were expelled from the city. "Well and good," said Calvin. "If we had served men we would have been ill-requited, but we serve a good Master who will reward us." Calvin retired to Strasbourg and a life of writing and preaching. He married a widow with two children, Idelette de Bure. In 1540, pressure from Roman Catholics and a near-riot prompted the town council of Geneva to recall Calvin as minister of the church and leader of the Reformation in the city. Calvin was in continual ill health. His wife's home was in Strasbourg, and he preferred to stay there. But in the end Farel's words rang in his ears, claiming that Calvin had a command from God to do this work. Calvin returned to Geneva and said to his congregation there:

> We are not our own: let not our reason and our will lord it over our counsels and our tasks. Let us not seek out

> what is expedient to the flesh. We are the Lord's: may every part of our life be referred to Him as to our only goal.

Although Calvin was conservative by temperament, upbringing, and conviction, his organizational ideas were among the most revolutionary in Europe. From his work came much of the structure of representative democracy we practice today in the Presbyterian Church.

Calvin as Practicing Christian

At the heart of Calvin's teaching was his understanding of *true piety.* In his first simple *Instruction in Faith* of 1537, Calvin wrote:

> True piety does not consist in a fear which willingly flees God's judgment, but since it cannot escape it is terrified. True piety consists rather in a sincere feeling which loves God as Father as much as it fears and reverences Him as Lord, embraces His righteousness, and dreads offending Him worse than death.

Piety, for Calvin, was love, loyalty, obedience, and service. Because it was centered on God, it was turned outward in service to the neighbor. Piety, for Calvin, was the root of love. Indeed, because God is higher than humans, piety was higher than love. Both were acted out in relations with one's neighbors. Calvin said that "believers seriously testify, by honoring mutual righteousness among themselves, that they honor God." Calvin stuck to his view even when it was difficult to honor and love those who were opposing him. Seeing himself in a moral situation parallel to David's in the Old Testament, Calvin wrote:

> David's condition was such that, deserving his people's esteem, he was nonetheless groundlessly hated by many. No small consolation to me it was—when assaulted by the unwarranted hatred of those who should have put

their efforts into helping me—to conform myself to such a great and excellent pattern.

For Calvin, true knowledge was evidenced by love of God and neighbor. "Indeed, we shall not say that, properly speaking, God is known where there is no religion or piety," Calvin proclaimed.

Calvin was human, with many human flaws. His judgment at times was faulty, as when he consented to the burning of the Unitarian, Michael Servetus. He used language we would consider intemperate and uncharitable. And he perhaps pushed people too fast and too far in his zeal for a perfect Christian community. But his sincerity and his sheer ability have made him a model for Reformed Protestants for centuries. And his scholarship, administrative capability, and sincere devotion are still qualities that Presbyterians esteem in their leaders.

An Appropriate Piety for the Present

A recent empirical study has probed present attitudes of church people on the relationship of faith and practice, truth and goodness. It indicates that concern for the characteristics evidenced by Calvin is still alive among Presbyterians. The Association of Theological Schools in the United States and Canada is the accrediting agency for institutions offering graduate theological education. For six years, between 1973 and 1979, it conducted a "Readiness for Ministry Project" to discover what congregations most wanted in their beginning ministers. Over 12,000 people, lay and clergy, participated. They responded to 1,200 general descriptions of ministry, 850 items describing specific actions of ministry, and 444 items that revealed patterns of ministry. From this data, analysts drew 64 dimensions of ministry and 11 key factors in ministry. All this has been published in a 500-page book entitled *Ministry in America.* Forty-seven denominations participated in the study, and the results were analyzed by denominational families, with Presbyterians among ten denominations in the Reformed family.

The responses of those in the Presbyterian/Reformed family of churches placed them right in the center of denominations in America. However, Presbyterians also showed "a distinctive emphasis on the importance of a learned grasp and presentation of Christianity," which are products of our historical heritage from Calvin and the Genevan Reformation. According to the study, Presbyterians want a minister to know "the historical circumstances that shaped the confessional statements of the denomination." The ideal of the minister as "theologian and thinker" lies at the center of the Presbyterian/Reformed self-image.

The study demonstrated that Presbyterians also believe in organization. "Presbyterian/Reformed respondents, more than the remaining group, tended to expect conscious planning by their leaders." According to this survey, Presbyterians "do *not* want pastors to substitute intuition and charisma for rational processes." Decency and order are not just slogans, they are values that Presbyterians expect their pastors to implement.

The central conclusion of this massive study shows that, in the end, people want a genuine integration of faith and practice in their pastors. The one quality congregations most often seek in their minister was described as an "open, affirming style." People want "a style of ministry that reflects a minister who is positive, open, flexible; who behaves responsibly to persons as well as tasks." That is not so different from what it has always been. When Calvin discussed the call to ministry in his *Institutes,* he asked, "Who can be a minister of this church?" His answer summed it up: "Only those are to be chosen who are of sound doctrine and of holy life, not notorious in any fault which might deprive them of authority and disgrace the ministry."

Presbyterians are people of three books. First is the Bible: It is the Word of God through which the Holy Spirit speaks to us of Jesus Christ on whom our faith is founded.

Second is *The Book of Confessions:* It reflects a Reformed range of responses to the Word of God. Third is *The Book of Order:* In it Presbyterians attempt to outline practical principles of obedience to the Word of God.

It is essential that we take all three of these books seriously. It is also necessary that we keep them in the right order of priority. In a time when our new church is restructuring its organization and rethinking its mission, it is essential that we renew our faith. We need to be Reformed, with a solid grasp on our confessional heritage. Then we will be able to be continually reforming, becoming more what God wants us to be in the present. Study of *The Book of Confessions* could aid immeasurably in that task. A knowledge of the truth and a genuine piety should support and structure our life in the church and our service in the world. Faith and practice, truth and goodness, still go together.

Resources for Further Study

Books Relating to Many of the Confessions

The Constitution of the Presbyterian Church (U.S.A.), Part I: The Book of Confessions. Office of the General Assembly, 1983.

Dowey, Edward A., Jr. *A Commentary on the Confession of 1967 and an Introduction to "The Book of Confessions."* Westminster Press, 1968.

Gerrish, Brian A., ed. *The Faith of Christendom: A Source Book of Creeds and Confessions.* World Publishing Co., 1963.

Keesecker, William F. *A Layperson's Study Guide to the Theology of the Book of Confessions of The United Presbyterian Church in the United States of America.* General Assembly of The United Presbyterian Church in the U.S.A., 1976.

Leith, John H., ed. *Creeds of the Churches: A Reader in Christian Doctrine from the Bible to the Present,* rev. ed. John Knox Press, 1973.

The Proposed Book of Confessions of the Presbyterian Church in the United States. General Assembly of the Presbyterian Church in the U.S. (Atlanta), 1976.

Chapter 1: A Church That Defines and Affirms Its Faith

The Constitution of the Presbyterian Church (U.S.A.), Part II: The Book of Order. Office of the General Assembly, 1983.

Rogers, Jack. "Setting the Margins." *The Presbyterian Outlook* (June 18, 1984): 18–19.

Chapter 2: From Scripture to Confessions of Faith

Leith, John H. *Introduction to the Reformed Tradition.* John Knox Press, 1977.

Routley, Erik. *Creeds and Confessions: From the Reformation to the Modern Church.* Westminster Press, 1963.

Vischer, Lukas, ed. *Reformed Witness Today: A Collection of Confessions and Statements of Faith Issued by Reformed Churches.* Evangelische Arbeitsstelle Oekumene Schweiz, 1982.

Chapter 3: The Nicene Creed

Historical Context

Athanasius. *Select Works and Letters.* Vol. IV of Select Library of Nicene and Post-Nicene Fathers, Series II; reprint. Wm. B. Eerdmans Publishing Co., 1971.

Ferm, Robert L. *Readings in the History of Christian Thought.* Holt, Rinehart & Winston, 1964.

Kelly, J.N.D. *Early Christian Doctrines,* rev. ed. Harper & Row, 1978.

Plantinga, Cornelius, Jr. *A Place to Stand: A Reformed Study of Creeds and Confessions.* Board of Publications of the Christian Reformed Church, 1979.

Rogers, Jack, Ross Mackenzie, and Louis Weeks. *Case Studies in Christ and Salvation.* Westminster Press, 1977.

Sayers, Dorothy. *The Emperor Constantine: A Chronicle.* Wm. B. Eerdmans Publishing Co., 1976.

Timiadis, Emilianos. *The Nicene Creed: Our Common Faith.* Fortress Press, 1983.

Contemporary Relevance

"On Affirmation of Deity and Humanity of Jesus Christ." *Minutes of the General Assembly of The United Presbyterian Church in the United States of America: Part I, Journal,* pp. 78–79. Office of the General Assembly (New York), 1981.

"Report of the Special Committee on the Work of the Holy Spirit" to the 182nd General Assembly of The United Presbyterian Church in the United States of America. Office of the General Assembly (Philadelphia), 1970.

"The Person and Work of the Holy Spirit with Special Reference to 'the Baptism of the Holy Spirit.'" (Action of the 1971 General Assembly) *Minutes of the 105th General Assembly of the Presbyterian Church in the United States,* pp. 174–178.

Thurian, Max, ed. *Ecumenical Perspectives on Baptism, Eucharist, and Ministry.* Faith and Order Paper 116. World Council of Churches, 1983.

Chapter 4: The Apostles' Creed

Historical Context

Kelly, J.N.D. *Early Christian Creeds,* 2nd ed. Longmans, Green & Co., 1960.

Rein, Gerhard, ed. *A New Look at the Apostles' Creed.* Tr. by David LeFort. Augsburg Publishing House, 1969.

Contemporary Relevance

"Committee Explains the New Inclusive Language Lectionary." *The Presbyterian Outlook* (Nov. 7, 1983): 4–5.

Frye, Roland Mushat, ed. *Is God a Creationist? The Religious Case Against Creation-Science.* Charles Scribner's Sons, 1983.

"One in Christ—'An Inclusive-Language Lectionary.'" National Council of Churches (Office of Information, 475 Riverside Drive, Room 850, New York, NY 10115), n.d.

The Power of Language Among the People of God and the Language About God "Opening the Door." United Presbyterian Church in the U.S.A., 1979.

Rogers, Jack. "Is God a Man?" *Theology, News and Notes* (June 1975): 3–4, 18.

Thompson, J. A. "Creation." In *The New Bible Dictionary,* ed. J. D. Douglas. Inter-Varsity Press, 1962.

Chapter 5: The Scots Confession

Historical Context

Berkouwer, Gerrit C. *Divine Election.* Tr. by Hugo Bekker. Wm. B. Eerdmans Publishing Co., 1960.

MacLeod, John. *Scottish Theology: In Relation to Church History.* Publications Committee of the Free Church of Scotland, 1943.
Murray, Ian. *John Knox.* Evangelical Library, 1973.
Ridley, Jasper. *John Knox.* Clarendon Press, 1968.

Contemporary Relevance

Naming the Unnamed: Sexual Harassment in the Church. Council on Women and the Church, United Presbyterian Church in the U.S.A., 1982.
Rassieur, Charles L. *The Problem Clergymen Don't Talk About.* Westminster Press, 1976.

Chapter 6: The Heidelberg Catechism

Historical Context

Hageman, Howard, ed. *Lily Among the Thorns.* Half Moon Press, 1953.
Plantinga, Cornelius, Jr. *A Place to Stand: A Reformed Study of Creeds and Confessions.* Board of Publications of the Christian Reformed Church, 1979.
Ursinus, Zacharias. *Commentary on the Heidelberg Catechism.* Tr. by G. W. Williard. Wm. B. Eerdmans Publishing Co., 1954.
Van Halsema, Thea B. *Three Men Came to Heidelberg.* Christian Reformed Publishing House, 1963.

Contemporary Relevance

Rogers, Jack B. "Ecological Theology: The Search for an Appropriate Theological Model." In *Septuagesimo Anno: Theologische Opstellen Aangeboden Aan Prof. Dr. G. C. Berkouwer.* J. H. Kok, 1973.
Rogers, Sharee and Jack. *The Family Together: Inter-Generational Education in the Church School.* Acton House, 1976.
Torrance, James. "Present Practice Obscures the Gospel." *Life and Work* (June 1979). Church of Scotland.
Weber, Hans-Ruedi. *Jesus and the Children: Biblical Resources for Study and Preaching.* John Knox Press, 1980.

Chapter 7: The Second Helvetic Confession

Historical Context

Bromiley, Geoffrey W., tr. *Zwingli and Bullinger.* Library of Christian Classics, Vol XXIV. Westminster Press, 1953.

Hillerbrand, Hans J., ed. *The Protestant Reformation.* Harper & Row, 1968.

Steinmetz, David. *Reformers in the Wings.* Fortress Press, 1971.

Contemporary Relevance

Loetscher, Lefferts A. "Presbyterian Church Property." *The Presbyterian Outlook* (Feb. 11, 1980): 5–7.

Miller, Allen O., ed. *A Covenant Challenge to Our Broken World.* Caribbean and North American Area Council, World Alliance of Reformed Churches, 1982.

"Report of the Permanent Committee on Conservation of Property." *Minutes of the 192nd General Assembly of The United Presbyrian Church in the United States of America: Part I, Journal,* pp. 99–105. Office of the General Assembly (New York), 1980.

Rogers, Jack. "The Three C's of Presbyterianism." *The Presbyterian Communique* (Spring 1982): 6–7.

Willis, David, ed. *Baptism: Decision and Growth.* General Assembly of The United Presbyterian Church in the U.S.A., 1972.

Chapter 8: The Westminster Confession of Faith and Catechisms

Historical Context

Leith, John H. *Assembly at Westminster: Reformed Theology in the Making.* John Knox Press, 1973.

Rogers, Jack Bartlett. *Scripture in the Westminster Confession: A Problem of Historical Interpretation for American Presbyterianism.* Wm. B. Eerdmans Publishing Co., 1967.

Rogers, Jack B., and Donald K. McKim. *The Authority and Interpretation of the Bible: An Historical Approach.* Harper & Row, 1979.

Contemporary Relevance

Biblical Authority and Interpretation. Advisory Council on Discipleship and Worship (475 Riverside Drive, Room 1020, New York, NY 10115), 1982.

Presbyterian Understanding and Use of Holy Scripture. Presbyterian Church (U.S.A.), Office of the General Assembly (Atlanta), 1983.

Ramm, Bernard. "Presbyterianism Springs Forth." *Eternity* (Nov. 1981): 49–51.

Chapter 9: The Theological Declaration of Barmen

Historical Context

Cochrane, Arthur C. *The Church's Confession Under Hitler.* Westminster Press, 1962.

Littell, Franklin H. *The German Phoenix: Men and Movements of the Church in Germany.* Doubleday & Co., 1960.

Shirer, William L. *The Rise and Fall of the Third Reich: A History of Nazi Germany.* Simon & Schuster, 1960.

Contemporary Relevance

"A Confessional Courage: The Life of Martin Niemoeller." *Sojourners* (Aug. 1981): 11–12.

Bilheimer, Robert S. "Martin Niemöller: Transcending Self." *The Christian Century* (Mar. 21–28, 1984): 296.

Kraft, Charles H. *Christianity in Culture.* Orbis Books, 1979.

Niebuhr, H. Richard. *Christ and Culture.* Harper & Row, 1951.

Rogers, Jack. "We Can Respond to Barmen." *The Presbyterian Outlook* (Apr. 30, 1984): 9–10.

Chapter 10: The Confession of 1967

Historical Context

"Assembly Confirms New Confessional Position." *Presbyterian Life* (June 15, 1967): 20–21.

"C67 Symposium Focus on Reconciliation and Liberation." *The Presbyterian Outlook* (Nov. 15, 1982): 3.

Dowey, Edward A., Jr. *A Commentary on the Confession of 1967 and an Introduction to "The Book of Confessions."* Westminster Press, 1968.

Hendry, George S. "The Bible in the Confession of 1967." *Princeton Seminary Bulletin* (Oct. 1966): 21–24.

"PUBC Meets in Chicago to Discuss 'Confession.'" *Presbyterian Life* (Jan. 1, 1966): 26–27.

"Presbyterians: The Layman Leader." *Time* (June 3, 1966): 60.

"Presbyteries Endorse Confessional Change." *Presbyterian Life* (Apr. 1, 1967): 24–25.

Reid, John Calvin. "Just How Different Is the 'Revised' Confession of 1967?" *Presbyterian Life* (Oct. 1, 1966): 34.

Report of the Special Committee on a Brief Contemporary Statement of Faith to the 177th General Assembly, The United Presbyterian Church in the United States of America, May 1965. Office of the General Assembly (Philadelphia), 1965.

Rogers, Jack B. "Biblical Authority and Confessional Change." *Journal of Presbyterian History* (Summer 1981): 131–159.

———. "The Kenyon Case." *Women and Men in Ministry: Collected Readings.* Ed. by Roberta Hestenes. Fuller Theological Seminary, 1980.

Contemporary Relevance

"Christian Faith and Economic Justice." *Minutes, 196th General Assembly, Presbyterian Church (U.S.A.): Part I, Journal,* pp. 363–413. Office of the General Assembly (Atlanta), 1984.

Commitment to Peacemaking. Presbyterian Distribution Center (905 Interchurch Center, 475 Riverside Drive, New York, NY 10115), n.d.

"Military Spending Has Human Cost." *Pasadena Star-News* (Oct. 8, 1983): 1–8.

Peacemaking: The Believers' Calling. Office of the General Assembly (New York), n.d.

"Reconciliation and Liberation—The Confession of 1967." *Journal of Presbyterian History* (Spring 1983): 1–196.

Sell, Alan. "What Is the World Alliance of Reformed Churches?" *The Presbyterian Outlook* (Sept. 10, 1984): 5.

"South Africa Churches Ousted." *Los Angeles Times* (Aug. 26, 1982): I, 2.

Chapter 11: Faith and Practice

Battles, Ford Lewis. *Analysis of the "Institutes of the Christian Religion" of John Calvin.* Baker Book House, 1980.

———, tr. and ed. *The Piety of John Calvin: An Anthology Illustrative of the Spirituality of the Reformer.* Music ed. by Stanley Tagg. Baker Book House, 1978.

Calvin, John. *Institutes of the Christian Religion.* Ed. by John T. McNeill. Tr. by Ford Lewis Battles. The Library of Christian Classics, Vols. XX and XXI. Westminster Press, 1960.

———. *Instruction in Faith (1537).* Ed. and tr. by Paul T. Fuhrmann. Westminster Press, 1949.

Kerr, Hugh T., ed. *A Compend of the Institutes of the Christian Religion by John Calvin.* Westminster Press, 1964.

McNeill, John T. *The History and Character of Calvinism.* Oxford University Press, 1967.

Parker, T.H.L. *John Calvin: A Biography.* Westminster Press, 1975.

Richard, Lucien Joseph. *The Spirituality of John Calvin.* John Knox Press, 1974.

Rogers, Jack. *Confessions of a Conservative Evangelical.* Westminster Press, 1974.

———. "Faith and Practice." *The Presbyterian Outlook* (Oct. 29, 1984): 10–11.

Strommen, Merton P., David S. Schuller, and Milo L. Brekke, eds. *Ministry in America.* Harper & Row, 1980.

Weeks, Louis B. *To Be a Presbyterian.* John Knox Press, 1983.